GYMNASTICS
Dan Gutman

Viking

Photos on pages xviii, 25, 40, 54, 56, 60, 61, 66, 68, 73, 75, 78, 86, 88, 90, 91, 93, 117, 121, 133, 135, 145, 149, and 156, and all photos in the color insert, courtesy of Dave Black. Photos on pages xv, xvi, 47, 99, 105, 107, 116, 118, 120, 129, 136, 143, 147, and 151, courtesy of Nancy Raymond. Photos on pages 14, 19, 50, 94, and 142, courtesy of the International Gymnastics Hall of Fame. Photo on page 30, courtesy of *International Gymnast*.

VIKING
Published by the Penguin Group
Penguin Books USA Inc., 375 Hudson Street, New York, New York 10014, U.S.A.
Penguin Books Ltd, 27 Wrights Lane, London W8 5TZ, England
Penguin Books Australia Ltd, Ringwood, Victoria, Australia
Penguin Books Canada Ltd, 10 Alcorn Avenue, Toronto, Ontario, Canada M4V 3B2
Penguin Books (N.Z.) Ltd, 182–190 Wairau Road, Auckland 10, New Zealand

Penguin Books Ltd, Registered Offices: Harmondsworth, Middlesex, England

First published in 1996 by Viking, a division of Penguin Books USA Inc.

1   3   5   7   9   10   8   6   4   2

LIBRARY OF CONGRESS CATALOGING-IN-PUBLICATION DATA
Gutman, Dan.
Gymnastics / by Dan Gutman.   p.   cm.
Includes bibliographical references and index.
Summary : Discusses the history, competitive events, and some superstars of gymnastics,
as well as problems and miscellaneous facts related to the sport.
ISBN 0-670-86949-X
1. Gymnastics—Juvenile Literature. [1. Gymnastics.]   1. Title.
GV461.G85 1996 796.44—dc20   95-50420   CIP   AC

Photographs by Dave Black (© Dave Black, 1995) and Nancy Raymond.
Reproduced by permission of the photographer.

Manufactured in U.S.A.
Set in Gill Sans

For Elizabeth Law

There is an instant after you have released your grip on the apparatus when you are in the air, free. There is no feeling like it. If you are trying some new technique there, in mid-air, you will know you have got it right. When you land you don't need applause or a medal—the satisfaction is inside you. You have conquered and it doesn't matter if it is in an empty hall. You have mastered fear, overcome difficulty. You are full of joy.

—Yuri Titov, Soviet gymnast and 1962 World Champion, in The Illustrated History of Gymnastics

ACKNOWLEDGMENTS

Many people helped gather the information that went into this book. Their assistance is greatly appreciated: Bruce Frederick and Glenn Sundby of the International Gymnastics Hall of Fame, Temple University gymnastics coach Fred Turoff, Nancy Raymond of *International Gymnast*, photographer Dave Black, Mary Salerno and Donna Strauss of Parkettes National Gymnastic Training Center in Allentown, Pennsylvania, Iris Gaughan of Rancocas Valley Regional High School, Amanda and Patty Borden, research assistants Brian Kearney and Boris Ginsburgs, Doug Raushenberg and the staff of the Haddonfield Public Library, Rich Tobin of the Gymnastics Academy in Cherry Hill, New Jersey, and Tom Forster of Colorado Aerials Gymnastics in Colorado Springs, Colorado.

Thanks also to Elizabeth Law, Regina Hayes, Nina Putignano, Margaret Mirabile, and Janet Pascal at Viking Children's Books, Liza Voges and Julie Alperen at Kirchoff/Wohlberg, Bob McCreary, Ike Richman of the CoreStates Spectrum in Philadelphia, Ron Sataloff, and Mark Schaeffer.

Finally, special thanks to my wife, Nina Wallace, who was nice enough to wait until this book was completed before going into labor with Emma.

CONTENTS

FOREWORD

There's a dusty chalk smell hanging in the air.

A young girl waits on the runway for the judge to give her the go-ahead. As she rolls her shoulders and shakes the nervous energy from her fingertips, she thinks back on how it began.

As far back as she could remember, she loved to jump, roll, flip, and fall. She'd walk on fences, curbs, or simply cracks in the sidewalk. She loved nothing better than to climb up things and jump off them, and then do it again. People said she was nuts.

She was five when she saw the Olympics on TV and first watched gymnasts throwing themselves around the bars, pommels, beam, and horse. She was instantly fascinated. She told her mom that she wanted to be in the Olympics someday.

Her mom took her to a gym and signed her up for a class. She fell all over the place in the beginning, but soon it became clear that she was better than the rest of the kids.

With good coaching, she got better still. She learned how to do incredible things, tricks that made people shake their heads with wonder.

She worked her tail off for ten years. She sacrificed a normal childhood for that one-in-a-million chance of making the Olympics. Her family sacrificed to give her the opportunity.

At times she thought about giving up gymnastics and just being a regular kid. But that dream of becoming an Olympian kept her going.

And now it all comes down to what she can make her body do in the next four seconds.

She knows in her head exactly what to do. She's done it a million times. The Tsukahara vault. She's going to sprint as fast as she can, leap on the springboard, rotate in the air, push off the horse as hard as she can, do a one-and-a-half back somersault in the air, and land facing the horse without taking a step.

Piece of cake.

If she does all that perfectly, they'll hang a gold medallion around her neck and play the national anthem. Maybe she'll become America's sweetheart. Maybe not. Mess up and she's next year's trivia question for sure.

Her face fills the screen on fifty million TV sets around the world. She tunes them out. She's learned to focus her concentration totally on the task at hand.

She jogs in place a little, closes her eyes to compose herself, and smacks her hands together. A hush falls over the crowd. She takes one deep breath.

And runs . . .

Introduction:
How to Speak Gymish

First Gymnast: How'd you do today?

Second Gymnast: Oh, man! I was doing great. I stuck a perfect flip-flop full, whip through to triple twist, two-and-a-half twist punch layout front and piked full-in, but then I messed up my Yurchenko and when I chucked a layout half-in half-out, I overrotated my piked barini and did a major face plant. How about you?

First Gymnast: Well, I rocked my Yamashita. But I was in the middle of a running double twisting flic-flac when I tried a punch front whipback double tuck flyspring. Big mistake! I overhyped my kip and had to do a front-full step-out to roundoff whip double twist dismount. Not only that, but on vault I missed the beat board and smashed into the croup. It seemed like I was eating mat all day.

Second Gymnast: Ouch! Tough meet. Well, see ya next week!

Like most sports, gymnastics has its own vocabulary. It sounds almost like a foreign language to people who don't know it. The following is a list of common gymnastics terms and what they mean.

You don't have to understand these definitions to enjoy this book. Almost all the terms in these pages are already familiar to you. But if you want to hang out at a gym and be one of the boys or girls, you might as well learn a little "gymish" . . .

Aerial: The gymnast turns over in the air without her hands or feet touching the apparatus.

Amplitude: Reaching the maximum height, extension, stretch, or swing for any movement.

Apparatus: The tools of gymnastics—pommel horse, bars, rings, and so on.

Arch: The body is curved backward. If the hands and feet are both on the ground, it's a "bridge" or a "crab."

Back-in, full-out: A double somersault with a twist in the second somersault. When the twist is in the first somersault, it's a "full-in, back-out." If there are two half twists, it's a "half-in, half-out."

Beat board: The springboard gymnasts use to begin their vault and uneven bars routines. Also called a "Reuther board."

Compulsories: Specific required exercises.

Crash pad: Thick mat to cushion falls.

Cross: On the rings, the arms are fully extended to each side, the body vertical. Also called an "iron cross" or "crucifix."

Croup: The part of the horse nearest the vaulter and to the right when facing the pommel. The opposite side of the horse is the "neck."

Diamidov: On the parallel bars, the gymnast turns 360 degrees from a handstand. Created by Sergei Diamidov of the Soviet Union.

Dislocation: The body hangs from a bar or rings with the arms behind the back.

Dismount: The last movement of a performance, when the gymnast flies from the apparatus to the ground.

Elite: A gymnast who has reached the highest level of the sport.

Face plant: When a gymnast falls flat on her face. Also called "eating mat."

F.I.G.: The International Federation of Gymnastics (Federation Internationale de Gymnastique).

Flic-flac: A back handspring. Also called a "flip-flop" or "back flip." Seen in floor exercises and on the balance beam.

Flip: A full rotation in the air (forward, backward, or sideways) without using the arms.

Flyspring: A handspring launched from both feet. Also called a "dive handspring."

Gaylord: On the high bar, the gymnast swings around the bar and does a one-and-a-half somersault before grasping the bar again. Created by American Mitch Gaylord.

Giant: The gymnast swings 360 degrees around the high bar, his body fully extended. Also called a "wheel."

Lu Li of China doing an inverted giant on the uneven bars.

Grips: Leather handguards gymnasts wear to reduce friction.

Handspring: The gymnast flips from her feet to her hands and back to her feet with a push from the shoulders.

Hip circle: The gymnast circles a bar with the body against it, at hip level.

Inverted hang: On the rings, the body is suspended upside down.

Kip: A movement that takes the gymnast from below the apparatus (usually bars) to above it.

Layout: The body is held straight or slightly arched.

Lever: The body is perfectly horizontal, supported by straight arms.

Mount: Getting up on the apparatus.

Tatiana Gutsu of the Ukraine doing a layout stepout mount on the beam.

Movement: One part of a routine.

Optionals: Routines in which the gymnast performs movements of her own choosing.

Pike: Legs held perfectly straight, body bent at hips, like a letter L.

Pipe: The horizontal bar or high bar.

Pirouette: Turning around while in a handstand.

Planche: The body is face down, horizontal, and supported entirely by the arms. *Planche* is French for "board."

Pommels: The handles on the top of the pommel horse.

Preflight: The part of the vault before the gymnast touches the horse.

Radochla: A somersault performed between the uneven bars.

Release: Letting go of a bar and then grasping it again.

Roundoff: The body turns at the height of a cartwheel, and the gymnast lands facing the direction she started.

Routine: A program, a performance, a combination of skills.

Saddle: The middle portion of the pommel horse.

Salto: A somersault.

Scale: Balancing on one leg or knee while holding the other leg in one of several positions. In a "Y-scale" she looks like the letter Y.

Scissors: Each leg swings alternately to the back and front of the pommel horse.

Side horse: Pommel horse.

Sissone: A jump which takes off from two feet and lands on one.

Sole circle: The body circles around a bar with both hands and feet on it.

Somersault: A forward, backward, or sideways flip.

Spot/Spotter: Standing by to help or catch the gymnast if she needs it. A person (usually the coach) who does this.

A coach spotting his student on the uneven bars.

Stalder: On the high bar, a giant swing with the legs straddled, body piked, moving into a handstand. Created by Josef Stalder of Switzerland.

Stick: To land cleanly, without taking a step. "I stuck it." Also called "nail," "hit," "rock," or "drill."

Straddle: Legs straight and wide apart.

Swan dive: The gymnast leaps from a standing position into a roll or handstand.

Trick: A movement or gymnastic skill.

Tsukahara: A vault in which the gymnast does a 180 degree turn on the way to the horse and a one-and-a-half somersault leaving it. Created by Mitsuo Tsukahara of Japan.

Tuck: Knees bent, legs held to the chest, body curled up like a ball.

Twist: The body rotates, with the spine remaining in one direction.

Undergrasp: Holding a bar with palms toward face. When the palms are turned away from the face, it's an overgrasp. When the palms are in opposite directions, it's a "mixed grip."

Walkover: A forward or backward movement in which the gymnast "walks" from feet to hands and back to feet. If the hands are not used, it's an "aerial walkover."

Whipback: A back handspring without using the hands.

Yamashita: A handspring vault with the body in pike position before landing. Created by Haruhiro Yamashita of Japan.

Yurchenko: A vault in which the gymnast does a round-off onto the springboard, back handspring onto the horse, and a twist or layout before landing. Created by Natalia Yurchenko of the Soviet Union.

The Fool Who Jumped
over a Bull

A long time ago—probably in ancient Greece—some fool jumped over a bull.

Another person happened to be watching, and said, "That looks like fun. I think I'll jump over that bull too, and I'll do it even *better.*"

A group of people gathered around to watch this curious activity, and soon they were shouting and cheering the two bull-jumping fools. This made the athletes want to jump even higher and farther and faster.

A few wise citizens were chosen to decide which one was better, and the athlete who was most successful at jumping over the bull was given a prize.

Soon there were bull-jumping contests all over the land. To make things more interesting, other events were added—swinging from tree branches, walking a tightrope, tumbling. The best athletes were cheered as heroes.

Actually, we'll never know exactly how the sport of gymnastics began. But we do know it is one of the oldest sports, around 2,500 years old. And the first "apparatus," historians believe, was the bull.

THE NAKED EXERCISE

At the start of a gymnastics meet at Penn State University in 1974, a gymnast named Jim Culhane shocked the crowd when he ran out on the floor wearing a mask.

That is, he was wearing *only* a mask. Otherwise, he was totally naked.

Culhane calmly did a roundoff, followed by a back handspring and a back somersault. Then he bowed to the audience and dashed for the exit, with campus policemen hot on his heels. The judges didn't give him a score, but Culhane certainly deserved a perfect 10.0 for the risk and originality of his performance.

Jim Culhane wasn't simply a crazed streaker. He was paying tribute to the original gymnasts who came 2,500 years before him.

In Greek, the word *gymnos* means "naked." Gymnastics literally means "exercising naked."

The ancient Greeks believed that physical fitness was important, and that men (not women) should strive for physical perfection. Every major city in Greece had an open-air gymnasium, complete with dressing rooms and baths. Athens had three—the Lyceum, the Academia, and the Cynosarges. Gymnasiums also functioned as schools where philosophy, literature, and music were taught. (In German-speaking countries, the term "gymnasium" is still used for schools for older students.) Plato and Aristotle held court in the gymnasiums.

Athletes—only men eighteen and over—practically lived in the gymnasiums. They trained there all day, every day. Tournaments were held in which athletes climbed ropes, ran races, wrestled, threw the javelin, and lifted weights. They performed in the nude, and women were forbidden to watch.

THE ANCIENT OLYMPICS

Women certainly have come a long way since the days of the ancient Greeks. In the first Olympics, in 776 B.C., the winner *received* a girl.

According to legend, King Oenomaüs offered his daughter Hippodamia in marriage to any man who could kidnap her and make a successful getaway by chariot (good qualities for a son-in-law, wouldn't you say?). Thirteen men tried. Each time, King Oenomaüs caught the young man and had him put to death.

The fourteenth man, Pelops, bribed someone to damage the axle of the king's chariot. He kidnapped Hippodamia one night and successfully outraced her father.

To celebrate, King Oenomaüs started the Olympic Games in Greece's valley of Olympia. As many as forty thousand spectators cheered on the athletes.

In the first few Olympics, all the events were footraces. Other events were eventually added, and some Olympics even had contests in music and poetry. The Games went on for five days. Winners received an olive wreath and returned home as heroes, receiving a free home, free meals for life, and large sums of money. The Olympics went on like this for centuries.

Women, of course, were not allowed to compete, or even *attend* the Olympic Games. If a woman was discovered at the competition, punishment was swift and severe—she was thrown off a cliff.

One time, a woman tried to sneak in. Her name was Pherenice

of Rhodes. She wore a disguise and came to the Games with her son, Pisidores, who was a boxer. When Pisidores won his competition, Pherenice ran to embrace him. That was when observers realized she was a woman. Pherenice, presumably, became the first Olympic cliff diver.

Greek history is full of art and writing that discusses the glory of gymnastics. Homer wrote about gymnastics in the *Iliad*, when he described how Achilles performed various athletic feats (of course, his biggest claim to fame was having a tendon named after him).

A painting in the Palace of Knossos shows a man vaulting over a bull. The fearless Greeks would grab the bull's horns (take the bull by the horns, you might say) and when the bull threw them, they would attempt to somersault up in the air and land on the bull's back.

Plato wrote in his classic book, *The Republic*, "Only he who joins the study of the muses with the gymnastic arts in the fairest proportions, may rightly be called the truly educated man."

The ancient Greeks, who celebrated physical perfection, made gymnastics a part of their everyday lives. The first modern Olympics were held in Athens one hundred years ago.

WHEN IN ROME . . .

In the second century, the Romans conquered Greece. They didn't care much about perfecting the human body. In fact, they were afraid that if the general public was *too* physically fit, people would be more likely to stage a revolution.

What the Romans cared about was building an army to fight wars. They constructed wooden horses, complete with a raised neck on one side and a real horse's tail at the other. Roman soldiers could practice mounting and dismounting from the horse without worrying about the reaction of a real horse.

The Olympic Games continued to be held during the Roman Empire, but in A.D. 393, Emperor Theodosius formally abolished them. Every able-bodied young man was needed for military service.

A 1,100 year tradition was over. Gymnasiums were closed. It would be many centuries until there would be any interest in gymnastics again.

JOUSTING GYMNASTS

During the Middle Ages, acrobats roamed from village to village performing gymnastic stunts and tumbling. They might put a tambourine on its side and walk on it as it rolled, or tie a rope between two trees and walk across it. But to some people, using the human body for acrobatics was a form of devil worship.

The most popular exercise in those days was jousting. Knights would charge toward one another on horses and fight with lances. While trying to stay on their horses—like gymnasts do today on the pommel horse—they had to knock somebody else off *his* horse.

5

According to legend, one German knight could leap over six horses wearing his full armor. And that, I suppose, was how the vault was created.

Interest in music, art, and culture was renewed during the Renaissance (fourteenth to seventeenth century). So was interest in physical development. To educate a boy, "Exercise his body continually," wrote Frenchman Jean-Jacques Rousseau. "Make him strong and healthy that you may make him wise and reasonable."

THE FATHER OF GYMNASTICS

"Modern" gymnastics began around 1800 when a German man named Johann Frederich Guts Muths developed a system of exercise based on what the Greeks had been doing centuries earlier. Muths added climbing, balance movements, and military drills. He also wrote the first real book on the subject, *Gymnastics for the Young* (1793), which was translated into many languages.

But the true father of gymnastics was a German professor named Frederick Ludwig Jahn (1778–1852). He opened the first modern gymnasium, near Berlin in 1811. The gym was outdoors and open to the sky, like the gyms of ancient Greece.

Germany had recently lost the Napoleonic Wars, and Jahn's aim was to strengthen the body so the Germans could defeat the French. To help accomplish his goal he created the parallel bars and pommel horse. He encouraged men to exercise twice a week.

It seems strange now, but Jahn's ideas were revolutionary at the time. Some people felt threatened by them. One of his followers was beaten to death. In July of 1819, Jahn was imprisoned. His gym was raided. The parallel bars were used for firewood.

Frederick Jahn spent six years in jail, but his followers spread gymnastics across Europe.

At the same time, a Swedish educator named Peter Henrik Ling (1776–1839) was developing his own system of physical exercise. But while Jahn felt strength training was most important, Ling's emphasis was on grace and form.

Ling created floor exercises for the Swedish army. As many as ten thousand men would perform these movements at the same time, much like today's calisthenics or aerobics classes.

Followers of Jahn and Ling debated for sixty years over which system made more sense. (Ling's supporters even claimed that parallel bars could deform the human body.) In the end, gymnastics evolved into a series of gymnastic events that combined the two ideas. Some events require great strength (rings, parallel bars); others emphasize grace (floor exercises, balance beam).

Meanwhile, gymnastic clubs were popping up all over Europe. By

Turn-of-the-century gymnastics included fencing, rope climbing, club swinging, and other events that seem strange to us now.

1860, there were two thousand in Germany alone. European immigrants were streaming to America, and they brought gymnastics with them. By the close of the 1800s, it had become a worldwide sport.

RETURN OF THE OLYMPICS

Fifteen centuries had gone by since the Emperor Theodosius of Rome had shut down the Olympic Games. The Roman Empire was long gone.

Sport had become a part of everyday life. People were playing games for fun and exercise, and spectators attended baseball, football, basketball, and soccer games for entertainment. The world was not at war (yet). A French nobleman named Baron Pierre de Coubertin convinced the nations of the world to revive the Olympics.

On April 6, 1896, the first modern Olympic Games were held—in Athens, fittingly. A two-thousand-year-old stadium was restored for the occasion. Nine sports were included, and gymnastics was one of them. Only seventy-five gymnasts from five nations bothered to attend. None of them were Americans, and none of them were women.

The Germans, who, after all, had developed gymnastics, won five gold medals in gymnastics in the first modern Olympics. Hermann Weingartner of Germany won the all-around title and the high bar, finished second on rings and pommel horse, and third on parallel bars.

There were some weird events in the early Olympics. Gymnastics officials didn't always agree on exactly what gymnastics should include. In some years, athletes had to know how to fence, wrestle, box, high jump, pole vault, or even heave a 110-pound weight.

Rope climbing was an Olympic gymnastics event from 1896 to 1932. Alberto Braglia of Italy was a terrific rope climber, and he won the all-around championship in the 1908 and 1912 Olympics.

Club swinging was an event in the 1904 and 1932 Olympics. Edward Hennig of the United States won the gold medal in 1904. Maybe the public didn't take to the event, but Hennig loved it. He was still swinging clubs into the 1950s. In fact, he won the United States championship in 1951, when he was seventy-one years old.

THE MODERN ERA

The middle of the century—1950—is a good place to date the beginning of present-day gymnastics, for three reasons: the Soviet Union, the Japanese, and women.

• The Soviet Union. The U.S.S.R. didn't enter the early Olympics. Maybe its athletes were too busy training. In the Soviet Union, the entire population would wake up and do exercises before they did anything else. In the workplace, factory floors stopped for ten minutes every morning so workers could exercise. After World War II, boarding schools sprang up across the country to train young gymnasts.

The Soviet Union entered the Olympics for the first time in 1952 in Helsinki, Finland, and won an incredible sixty-nine medals. Five of the top seven male gymnasts were Soviets, as were seven of the top nine women. It was the beginning of a long streak of Soviet domination. The Soviets would win the women's team title in every Olympic Games from 1952 to 1976.

• The Japanese. Japan was barred from the 1948 Olympics because of the country's role in World War II. In 1950, the United States sent three gymnasts to Tokyo on a goodwill tour. The Japanese filmed everything they saw and their top gymnasts quickly began learning how to perform the same tricks.

In 1952, the Japanese were the laughingstock of the Olympics. But their men finished second as a team in 1956. In the 1960 Olympics, showing off the fluid and technically perfect routines they were now known for, they won the gold medal. They won it again in 1964. And again in 1968. And 1972.

As a group, the Japanese men were—and perhaps still are—the best gymnasts in the world.

• Women. Up until this point women hadn't played a big part in the history of gymnastics. They were not even allowed to compete until the 1928 Olympics in Amsterdam. Even then, there was only an all-around team competition. Women did not compete in individual events until the 1952 Olympics.

At first, women's gymnastics was an imitation of men's gymnastics. But gradually, the women stopped trying to show how strong they were and began focusing on grace, fluid movement, and perfect form. Women began to incorporate ballet and dance into their performances. In 1956, the German women's team withdrew from the Olympics, in protest against the new emphasis on graceful movement. (Germany returned, of course, and Karin Janz won two gold medals at the 1972 Olympics.)

Gradually it has become evident that gymnastics is one of the few sports (figure skating is another one) in which people prefer watching female athletes compete to watching male athletes.

Once they were thrown off cliffs for even attending the Olympics. Today, women gymnasts command higher TV ratings, more prize money, more endorsements, and more attention than the men.

———

Despite gymnastics' 2,500-year history, it was still a little-known fringe sport until quite recently. "To most Americans," *Life* magazine wrote in 1958, "gymnastics is an athletic ritual pursued by crackpots, musclebound culturalists and misguided persons named Ivan."

But then a little girl came along who turned everything upside down . . .

2

The First Superstars

OLGA KORBUT

"Gymnastics is an expression of my innermost emotions, my response to the love and care with which I have always been surrounded in my life."

When she walked into the Sporthalle in Munich, Germany on August 27, 1972, people thought she was somebody's assistant, or maybe a coach's daughter. She was seventeen years old, but at 4′11″ and 85 pounds, Olga Korbut looked barely twelve.

With strips of yarn holding her wild blond pigtails in place, she didn't look much like a gymnast. She certainly didn't look like her serious Soviet teammates, with their classical, flowing, balletic grace.

But when one of those teammates became injured just before the Olympics, Olga Korbut got the call to join the Soviet team.

Almost immediately, the crowd in Munich, and millions of people gathered around television sets worldwide, sensed Olga Korbut was something different. She was natural and spontaneous. She had a fresh energy, innocence. She would actually *smile* at the audience! Personality and charm burst out of her. She was a little sparrow, an imp.

More than all that, she could *fly*. In the days before the perfect ten had been attained, Olga scored a 9.7 on the vault and a 9.75 on the floor exercise. Going into the fourth day of the Olympics, she had helped the Soviet Union win the team gold medal and was in third place in the all-around, just .15 from first place.

Then, disaster struck. Jumping on to start her uneven bars routine, Olga bobbled momentarily. It threw off her timing. A few seconds later, performing a simple glide kip, she stubbed her toe. That made things worse. She tried to recover her rhythm, but she was hurrying and committed other glaring errors.

Disgusted, Olga dismounted. There was no need to look at the scores. She had botched the routine and she knew it. The crowd gasped when the scoreboard showed 7.5. Olga had fallen out of medal contention.

Experienced gymnasts are trained to keep their emotions in check, and the Soviets in particular had a reputation for looking stern and robotic. But Olga slumped into a chair, covered her eyes, and began sobbing. A hush fell over the crowd. This wasn't crying for the television cameras. It was a little girl responding to the moment and crying her eyes out.

A spectator ran over and handed Olga a bouquet of flowers. That only seemed to make it worse. All over the world, hearts were melting. "The Soviets actually cry!" people were thinking. "The Soviets actually have *feelings*!"

Olga probably would have preferred to slink back to her parents' home in Grodno, near the border of Poland. But the individual apparatus events would be the very next day, and she was a part of the team now.

The whole world, it seemed, tuned in just to watch her. What they saw was Olympic history.

Olga calmly mounted the balance beam and performed the first backflip ever—a frighteningly daring move back then. She got on the uneven bars and did a backflip off the high bar. With her incredibly flexible spine, she did impossible-looking contortions on the floor exercises.

Olga Korbut performs a perfect stag handstand.

In the end, Olga won the gold medal on the beam, another gold on the floor, and a silver on the uneven bars. She stole the show from the favorite, teammate Ludmilla Tourischeva.

Thanks to the power of television, the story of Olga's rise and fall and eventual triumph captured the imagination of the world. In five days she was transformed from a complete unknown into the most famous woman in the world.

The press dubbed her "the Munchkin of Munich" and followed her around the Olympic village hoping to find out all about her. It was news when Olga said she would eat a bottle of ketchup in a meal. People thought it was adorable when she told a reporter, "Life is marvelous now because I have a tape recorder."

Olga received thousands of fan letters, some of them simply addressed, "Olga, Moscow." She was invited to the White House. She met the queen of England. Better still, she met Mickey Mouse.

Olga was so popular, she *became* gymnastics. Shortly after the Olympics, the International Gymnastics Federation tried to ban Olga's new trick—the double backward somersault on the balance beam—because they believed it was too dangerous.

"If the decision is put into effect," Olga said, "I simply do not see any place for myself in gymnastics."

Very quickly, any discussion of banning daring moves stopped.

Gymnastics, because of the interest in Olga Korbut, became a "real" sport. Thousands of gymnastics clubs opened in America and in other countries where gymnastics had been virtually unknown. Before Olga, there were 15,000 practicing gymnasts in America. Ten years later there would be 150,000.

———

Olga went back to Grodno after the Olympics and went to college there. She retired from gymnastics in 1977, at age twenty-two.

She happened to meet Russian rock singer Leonid Bartkevich on a plane and soon the pair got married. They moved to Minsk, where Olga became a gymnastics coach. She also worked to benefit victims of the 1986 Chernobyl nuclear disaster.

When the International Gymnastics Hall of Fame opened in 1987, Olga Korbut was the first inductee. In 1994 *Sports Illustrated* chose forty people who have had the most impact on sports in the last forty years. Olga was one of only four women on the list, and the only gymnast.

Today, Olga and Leonid live in Atlanta with their teenage son, Richard.

Four years after her triumph in Munich, Olga Korbut was named captain of the Soviet team and she returned to the Olympics to defend her titles. She won a silver medal on the balance beam and a gold medal for being a member of the Soviet team.

But in the fast-moving world of gymnastics, Olga's time in the spotlight was over. By 1976, another young woman—an even *younger* woman—would capture the world's imagination.

NADIA COMANECI

"I was never thinking of the score. You can't. You can't think, 'Oh, I want to have a ten.' What do you win after this? Nothing. You must do the exercise, because the score will come."

Onesti, Romania, 1968. It was recess in an elementary school playground. Kindergarten kids were running all over the place. Two little girls were turning cartwheels and doing handstands.

A man named Bela Karolyi happened to be watching. He had been instructed to start a national school of gymnastics and was traveling by bicycle from school to school searching for kids who might have ability.

Karolyi caught sight of the two girls for a moment. But just as he was about to go over to them, a school bell rang and the children all scampered inside. The little girls were gone.

He rushed inside the school. Like the prince in the story of Cinderella, he went from class to class trying to find the tiny gymnasts.

Finally, in one class, Karolyi noticed a little six-year-old blond-haired girl looking at him out of the corner of her eye. Karolyi asked the girl if she could do a cartwheel. It was as if the prince had asked Cinderella to try on the glass slipper.

The girl did a perfect cartwheel.

Of course she did. Her name was Nadia Comaneci.*

Romania was not a gymnastics powerhouse at the time, having won just two bronze medals in the nation's history. The government decided to do something about that, and sixty Romanian children—some as young as six years old—were plucked away from their families to train at Karolyi's school. In return, they received free food, lodging, and education.

It wasn't easy. Karolyi treated these tiny girls like they were professional football players. They worked out for several hours twice a day, often seven days a week. He was tough, yelling and humiliating them when they made mistakes. Sometimes that helped motivate the kids. Other times it reduced them to tears.

---

* The other girl Karolyi spotted, Viorica Dumitro, would become one of Romania's best ballerinas.

Nadia placed thirteenth in her first competition. She was not the best of the young girls, but she worked harder than all the others. When Karolyi asked her to do something, she never said "No" or "I can't do that." She would always give it her best try.

By the time she was eight years old, Nadia was the Romanian junior champion. At eleven, she was the best gymnast in the country. At thirteen, she was tops in Europe. Just fourteen in 1976, she was good enough to be turned loose on the world.

As they marched into the arena in Montreal on July 18, 1976, the Romanian team looked like a bunch of elves. The entire group was outfitted with white leotards, red piping and pigtails held in place by red and white bows. They were all about Nadia's size—4'11", 85 pounds.

The Soviet women's team, captained by a mature twenty-one-year-old Olga Korbut, was expected to dominate the Olympics as they usually did.

But from that first day of competition, it was clear that Korbut was out and Comaneci was in. Nadia showed precision and daring that went far beyond anything Olga had accomplished four years earlier.

Nadia was throwing tricks no woman had ever attempted—double twists, double backward somersaults. Her "Salto Comaneci" was a dismount off the uneven bars with a half twist into a back somersault. Her piked back somersault off the vault rivaled the one by Mitsuo Tsukahara, and he invented it.

She landed all these tricks consistently, with a style, strength and confidence that fourteen-year-old girls were not supposed to have. Observers were left gasping, then cheering.

———

*Nadia Comaneci's trademark end pose for her floor exercise
at the 1976 Olympics.*

That first day of the Olympics, Nadia finished a spectacular compulsory uneven bars program. A few seconds passed and the scoreboard flashed 1.0.

"Where is Nadia's score?" the easily angered Bela Karolyi asked the judges. Just then, an announcement came over the public address system . . .

"Ladies and gentlemen, for the very first time in Olympic history, Nadia Comaneci has received the score of a perfect ten!"

Perfect. Nobody's perfect. People are only *human.* Humans make *mistakes.* We're *flawed* creatures. But this cute little girl from Romania had achieved perfection. It was unbelievable.

People started believing the next night, when Nadia scored another ten on the uneven bars as well as a ten on the balance beam.

By the end of the competition, she had reeled off *seven* perfect scores. That was good enough to win the all-around championship, a gold medal on the beam, a second gold on the uneven bars, a bronze for her floor exercises, and a silver for being a member of the second-place Romanian team.

While Olga Korbut watched, gymnastics gained a new sweetheart.

Nadia was very different from Olga. She didn't smile or flirt with the crowd. She kept her emotions hidden. She didn't seem to notice (or care) that 50 million people were watching her every move.

Comaneci shunned publicity, so the Nadia-starved public only heard dribs and drabs of information about her. She never ate bread or sugar, but she liked yogurt. She had collected more than one hundred dolls in their national costumes, and kept one of them on the bench for good luck. She didn't have many friends. She claimed she never cried.

The less Nadia revealed, the more people wanted to know. One reporter asked her what her greatest wish was, and she replied, "I want to go home."

Nadia was mysterious. She was the Greta Garbo of gymnastics.

Just as they had with Olga Korbut four years earlier, some members of the gymnastics establishment called for Nadia's more daring tricks to be banned. They were afraid that gymnasts would get hurt trying to duplicate them.

(They were right. Gymnasts *would* get hurt. See Chapter 7.)

But it was too late. The revolution had already started. Little girls all over the world began flinging themselves over couches, off railings, and through monkey bars. These girls went on to become the champions of the 1990s.

One Sunday morning shortly after the Olympics, Bela Karolyi went to the gym to conduct practice, but nobody was around. He searched all over to see if the girls might be hiding, which they sometimes did to play a trick on him.

As it turned out, the entire team had been taken away and moved to Bucharest, the capital of Romania. The government was now running the famous Romanian gymnastics team.

Gymnastics is a sport in which the athlete must train almost constantly to remain competitive. Without Karolyi's strict training regimen, Nadia and the other Romanian girls fell out of shape.

In 1977 and 1978, Nadia began losing competitions. Sometimes she didn't even show up to compete. She had developed a sweet tooth, and American gymnasts reported that she would slip them twenty-dollar bills and whisper what kind of junk food she wanted them to get her. She gained an astonishing forty pounds.

"I was like an elephant," she said later.

To make things worse, Nadia went on crash diets to lose the weight. At one point, she stopped eating entirely. Word got out, and the disease we now call anorexia was sometimes referred to as "Nadia syndrome."

At the same time, Nadia was going through the natural body changes of puberty, which is tough on every kid. There were rumors that she was being given "brake drugs" to slow her development.

Nadia lost her world title. She was only sixteen years old, but she talked of retiring from gymnastics. Later, Bela Karolyi revealed that Nadia had attempted to commit suicide by drinking liquid detergent.

Five weeks before the 1978 World Championships, Bela Karolyi was sitting in his hotel room when there was a knock at the door. It was Nadia. Karolyi could barely recognize her. She looked like she was twice her previous size.

"I want to go back with you," Nadia begged. "I hate myself. I hate everybody. I want to die."

Karolyi agreed to take Nadia on, and he proceeded to work her like a horse. He had her running night and day. He put her on a strict diet. He found out who was smuggling her chocolate and got rid of him.

In a few weeks, Nadia had shed thirty-five pounds. She wasn't in top shape in time for the World Championships, but she still managed to win on the balance beam.

By the time the 1980 Olympics arrived, Nadia was back in competition form. She was no longer a fragile, fourteen-year-old elf. She was a nineteen-year-old woman. Three and a half inches taller and twenty-one pounds heavier, she had curves where her body once had straight lines.

But she wasn't fat. She was lean, sleek, muscled, and catlike. She even had a more mature haircut.

Once again, Nadia was the star of the Olympic Games. She took the gold medal for the balance beam and the floor exercise. Between her Olympic and World Championships, Comaneci had won twenty-one gold medals.

As a national treasure of Romania, Nadia was watched carefully by the Communist government. Under Communist rule, the Romanian government placed tight restrictions on travel and emigration. When Bela Karolyi defected in 1981, remaining in the United States after an exhibition tour with the Romanian team, he was breaking Romanian law. There was concern that Nadia might follow him. She received frequent requests to make personal appearances in non-Communist countries, but she was not allowed to go. She was under constant surveillance by the secret police.

Nadia planned to compete in the 1984 Olympics in Los Angeles, but six weeks before the games she changed her mind and retired from gymnastics. She was twenty-two.

From 1984 to 1989, Nadia Comaneci didn't turn a single cartwheel. She accepted a government coaching job for twenty dollars a month. The free world heard little about her. She was invited to be an honored guest at the 1988 Olympics in Korea, but the Romanian government would not allow her to go.

By 1989, Nadia decided she had taken enough. With the help of a Romanian emigré from America named Constantin Panait, she fled Romania. Nadia had to walk for six hours in the middle of the night, making her way past barking dogs, armed guards, and barbed wire. Finally, she made it to an opening in the fence at the Hungarian border.

Panait brought her to the United States, where they landed at Kennedy airport on November 28, 1989. "I like life," Nadia whispered at the press conference there. "I want to have a free life."

But Nadia was not quite free. She spoke virtually no English and had to rely on Panait for everything.

Constantin Panait, it turned out, had other motives than gaining freedom for Nadia. He encouraged Nadia to perform again, but kept her fees for exhibitions and endorsements. He threatened to have her deported if she let anybody know.

Basically, he was holding her hostage.

Word about Nadia's situation began getting around, and two people came to her aid—former Romanian rugby coach Alexandru Stefu and American gymnast Bart Connor. They lured Panait to a meeting, promising a big payday for Nadia. When Panait showed up, they accused him of controlling Nadia and taking her money. Panait fled and Comaneci wasn't bothered by him again.

Nadia and Bart Connor had first met fourteen years earlier, when they were the male and female winners at the American Cup gymnastics meet in New York City. He was eighteen and she was fourteen at the time. The two shared an innocent kiss for photographers as they held their trophies aloft.

When Bart helped Nadia get free from Constantin Panait, the two kissed again. This time sparks flew. There was no public announcement, but everyone in gymnastics knew that two of the most famous gymnasts were boyfriend and girlfriend.

November 12, 1994 was Nadia's thirty-third birthday. She and Bart were in Amsterdam on their way to the World Champi-

Bart Connor—who would become Nadia's husband—winning the gold medal on the parallel bars at the 1984 Olympics.

onships when Bart suddenly proposed marriage.

Stunned, Nadia replied, "No." But then she thought it over for a few minutes and changed her mind. The happy couple went to Romania so Bart could personally ask Nadia's father Gheorghe, a car mechanic, for his daughter's hand in marriage.

Today, Nadia and Bart are a sort of "Fred and Ginger" of gymnastics. They perform together at exhibitions around the world. They run the Bart Connor Gymnastics Academy in Norman, Oklahoma. They raise money for charities such as United Cerebral Palsy. You may have seen Nadia in endorsements for 3M, Coca-Cola, and Jockey For Her underwear.

After all she had been through, Nadia Comaneci became bigger than ever in the 1990s—the shy little girl from Romania was 90 feet long across a billboard in the middle of Times Square.

THE AMERICAN REVOLUTION

For most of the twentieth century, the United States was the laughingstock of the gymnastics world. But at the 1932 Olympics in Los Angeles, the U.S. surprised everybody.

George Gulack won the gold medal on the rings. Gulack was born in Latvia in 1905. He took up gymnastics at twelve, when Germany invaded his hometown of Riga and made it a part of his school curriculum. Gulack was a sixteen-year-old champion when his family moved to the United States.

One of the first things Gulack did when he arrived in New York City was to look in the Manhattan phone book for a gym. He found one at Eighty-fifth Street and Lexington Avenue and joined it. Soon he was winning tournaments and became the national champion. He won the 1932 Olympic gold for rings easily, and another American, William Denton, won the silver.

In Indian club swinging, club swingers would twirl clubs shaped like bowling pins around themselves for four minutes, being careful not to let the clubs touch each other or their bodies. This strange sport was a part of gymnastics in 1932, and George Roth was the best in the world.

Roth's father died when George was nine, and his mother a few years later. The remaining family was dirt poor, and Roth claimed that he once went fifteen days without food. The Olympics would not make him rich. Roth had to hitchhike to the arena to pick up his gold medal. And when the ceremony was over, he hitched a ride back home.

Altogether, the United States took home five gold medals for gymnastics that year. Dallas Bixler won on horizontal bar. Rowland Wolfe won for tumbling. Raymond Bass won for rope climbing, which is no longer an Olympic event, but is practiced in millions of gym classes.

After 1932, America dropped back out of the medal race for many years. How bad was the U.S.A.? In the 1956 Olympics, only one American man was among the top thirty. Not a single American woman was among the top fifty.

Things started to change in the 1970s. Cathy Rigby won the silver on the balance beam at the 1970 World Championships. At the 1976 Olympics, Peter Kormann took the bronze in floor exercise. Marcia Frederick won a gold medal in the uneven bars at the 1978 World Championships.

At the same competition, American Kurt Thomas won a gold in the floor exercise. He was America's first great male gymnast.

KURT THOMAS

"Ninety percent of gymnastics is the mental ability to perform when the time comes."

Male gymnasts used to come from the field of body building and wrestling. They were big, heavy, musclebound lugs who liked to pose and flex and see how long they could hold an iron cross on the rings.

Kurt Thomas was not big. As a boy, in fact, he was so small and thin that his mother was concerned that he might be a midget.

When Kurt was nine, she took him to a genetics specialist at a hospital in Miami, where they lived. The doctor didn't find any growth abnormality, but he did find a heart murmur. Kurt was to be watched carefully for five years.

Kurt loved sports, but he was too small to play basketball, football, or baseball. At thirteen, he was only 4'9" and 77 pounds.

He didn't live in a good neighborhood to be small and skinny. Two of his friends at Miami Central High School were shot while walking home from school. Kurt's dad was hit by a car and killed when Kurt was seven. To avoid getting beaten up or robbed, Kurt hired his older sister to accompany him on his paper route. In high school he had a football player walk around with him and protect him.

One day when Kurt was fourteen, he saw a gymnast at Miami-Dade Junior College practicing on the high bar. The guy wasn't much bigger than Kurt.

"I used to like to swing on the monkey bars in the playground as a little kid," he remembered. "So I figured I'd try gymnastics." Coincidentally, the high school gym teacher was starting a gymnastics team.

When Kurt showed up for the first class, the teacher took one look at him and told him to go home. He was just too small and light for a "he-man" sport like gymnastics.

Thomas went home, but he came right back for the first practice the next Monday. The teacher let him stay. The little runt may not have had the muscle, but he had the motivation. And when the teacher asked all the boys to do a handstand, Kurt was the only one who could do it.

Quickly, the teacher realized Kurt had real talent for gymnastics. He had what is called a great "air sense." He always seemed to land on his feet, like a cat.

His muscles began to fill out and the heart murmur disappeared. In May of his freshman year, Kurt finished third in the regionals of the Junior Olympics. In his sophomore year, nobody could beat him.

Kurt reached his full adult size—5'5", 127 pounds with short legs and long arms. As people were beginning to discover, that is just about the *perfect* size for a male gymnast.

Very heavy men can't hoist themselves around the apparatus. Very tall men get their legs tangled up in the rings, pommels, and parallel bars. Being small gives the gymnast a lower center of gravity and greater strength in proportion to his weight.

After high school, Kurt entered Indiana State University. He became a serious gymnast there, going through grueling two-hour workouts three times a day.

One of his classmates, basketball player Larry Bird, received much more attention than Kurt. But Kurt was gaining a reputation as one of the best in his sport. He had a clean-cut, fresh-scrubbed look, and he would be mobbed by young girls after competitions. One fifteen-year-old girl ran away from home and showed up on Kurt's doorstep, hoping she could live with him.

That didn't sit well with Kurt's wife, Beth. The two had met at a sorority party and got married on one of the few days he wasn't training. While Larry Bird was getting 3 million dollars to play in the NBA, Beth and Kurt lived in a trailer. Beth held down two jobs to support them.

Kurt was still in college when he created the trick that made him famous—"The Thomas Flair." On the pommel horse he would suddenly fly into a series of wide-swinging leg moves in which he would kick his feet high up in the air. He introduced the technique at Barcelona in 1975.

Kurt Thomas demonstrates the "Thomas Flair" on the pommel horse. He also did this move in his floor exercise.

"It's kind of like a helicopter," he explained. "My legs whirl and then I go into a scissors." *Sports Illustrated* wrote that Kurt looked "as if blown around the horse by a giant fan."

Kurt Thomas became one of the few Americans to have a gymnastics trick named after him. He also began doing the Thomas Flair right on the mat in the middle of his floor exercise.

Kurt made the 1976 United States Olympic team, and thanks to the Flair was favored to win the gold medal on the pommel horse. But a few days before the Olympics he got hurt, damaging the ligaments in his right index finger.

Kurt didn't win anything. He finished twenty-first in the all-around. He was devastated. That October he cut the same hand opening a can of beans and needed fourteen stitches to sew it up.

Kurt could have called it quits right there and moved on with his life, but he loved gymnastics and wasn't ready to let it go. He decided to make an all-out effort to dedicate himself to the *next* Olympics, in Moscow in 1980.

His efforts seemed to be paying off. In the 1978 World Championships, he won the gold medal for the floor exercise. That made him the first American in forty-six years to win an international gymnastic event. In the all-around event, he was sixth best in the world.

He was even better in 1979. In the World Championships, Kurt took the gold for high bar, gold for floor exercises, silver for parallel bars, silver for pommel horse, and silver for the all-around championship.

For the first time in four decades, an American gymnast was as good as—if not better than—anyone else in the world.

"For so long, our flag has been down in the box somewhere during the medal ceremonies," said Kurt. "Now it was up there almost every time. It was a great feeling."

Kurt Thomas was putting men's gymnastics on the map, just as Olga Korbut had done for women's gymnastics. His picture started popping up on magazine covers. He appeared on *The Tonight Show*.

Kurt was reaching his athletic peak right on schedule to dominate the Olympics. And America hadn't won a gold medal in gymnastics since 1932.

"His eyes are fixed firmly on the gold that will dangle in Moscow next year," reported *The New York Times*.

"If he wins the gold medal in Moscow," one Hollywood agent said, "Kurt Thomas will be the biggest thing to hit this country since Neil Armstrong."

Then one night early in 1980 Kurt was reading and Beth was watching TV when she said, "Kurt, you better watch this. It's about the Olympics."

Kurt put down his book and heard the news—President Carter had announced that the United States was going to boycott the 1980 Olympics unless the the Soviet Union withdrew its troops from Afghanistan by February 20.

The Soviets had no intention of pulling out. They announced that they would hold the Olympics in Moscow whether the United States showed up or not.

For the second time, the Olympic dreams of Kurt Thomas (and hundreds of other athletes) were shattered. He had trained so hard for so many years, and would not have the chance to get an Olympic medal draped around his neck.

Angry and disgusted, Kurt retired from gymnastics. He got a few offers to do commercials and starred in a laughably bad movie called *Gymkata* (see Chapter 9). There was a Las Vegas–style gymnastics show. He did some TV commentary during the 1984 Olympics. Mostly, he served as a gymnastics coach at Arizona State University.

When athletes lose fair and square, they can usually handle it. But to be perhaps the best in the world, on the brink of glory, and then have it snatched away, can be tough on anybody.

Kurt and Beth's marriage couldn't survive it, and they divorced. In 1989, Kurt filed for bankruptcy.

Kurt's quest for Olympic gold was eating at him, and that November the gymnastics world was shocked by the announcement that he would be attempting a comeback. He said he wanted to win a medal at the 1992 Olympics in Barcelona.

It sounded crazy. Kurt would be thirty-six years old, which is *ancient* for a gymnast. He would be ten years away from his world titles and fifteen years older than some of the gymnasts he would be competing against.

It wasn't crazy. Just unreasonable. Gymnastics is a sport for the young. A thirty-six-year-old body simply can't take the pounding punishment dished out by the vault, the pommel horse, the bars, and the floor exercises.

During the Olympic trials, he hurt his ankle landing a vault, and then damaged his shoulder and wrist. He finished sixteenth, and finally realized his career as a competitive gymnast was over.

While Kurt Thomas's career may have been finished, something good had come from it. Now there were *dozens* of short, compact, and incredibly talented American male gymnasts who were good enough to compete with the Soviets, the Japanese, and anyone else in the world.

Kurt Thomas never won an Olympic medal, but these younger men would. And they had been inspired to take up gymnastics when they saw the heights Kurt Thomas achieved in his prime.

MARY LOU RETTON

"At night sometimes I dream gymnastic dreams. I'll be lying there quietly, sound asleep, and suddenly my whole body will give a great big jump and practically throw me out of bed."

As soon as Mary Lou Retton could walk, she started running around, bouncing off the walls, and causing trouble. Her mother, Lois, nicknamed her "the Great Table Smasher and Lamp Toppler."

"I was very hyper," Mary Lou says.

"Retton" is a shortened version of the Italian name "Rettundo," which means "round." Mary Lou was born in Fairmont, a coal-mining town in northern West Virginia. She was a pretty normal kid with a collie named Tarzan and a collection of stuffed lambs. She hated wearing dresses and was considered to be a tomboy.

The Rettons were an athletic family. Mary Lou's dad, Ron, played alongside basketball great Jerry West at West Virginia University. He went on to play minor league baseball in the New York Yankees organization. Mary Lou's three older brothers played baseball, basketball, and football. Her older sister Shari was an All-American gymnast.

Ron and Lois Retton thought that dancing school might help the Great Table Smasher burn off some energy. Mary Lou took tap, ballet, and acrobatics lessons. She was eight when she watched Nadia Comaneci score all those perfect tens on TV at the 1976 Olympics.

For Mary Lou, that was it. Gymnastics became her life.

In her first competition, as an eight-year-old, Mary Lou finished her routine and raced around the gym gleefully. She was sure she had received a perfect ten. Then somebody informed her that her score was 1.0, not 10.0.

But she progressed quickly. Soon she was getting those tens and winning competitions. She was a natural, and there aren't many naturals in gymnastics.

By the time she was twelve, Mary Lou was the best gymnast in West Virginia, and the only elite gymnast in the state. She realized she had a shot at making the 1984 Olympic team.

She also realized, however, that there were a lot of flaws in her gymnastics. Her coach, Gary Rafaloski, was good, but he was a quiet, easygoing man. Mary Lou felt she needed to be pushed by a more forceful personality in order to reach the Olympics, which were to be held in Los Angeles.

Enter Bela Karolyi.

During a 1982 competition in Salt Lake City, Utah, Mary Lou met Karolyi, the Romanian coach who helped Nadia Comaneci achieve greatness. Karolyi had recently moved to the United States and would soon be opening a gym in Houston, Texas.

Mary Lou asked him if he would coach her, and Karolyi said he would. She would have to move to Texas, though.

"I knew that if I didn't go, I'd never really know whether I could have made it to the Olympics," says Mary Lou.

The Rettons had a family meeting to discuss whether Mary Lou was mature enough to handle the responsibility of being on her own. Her parents decided it was a once-in-a-lifetime opportunity and gave her their blessing to leave home and live in Houston.

Mary Lou couldn't bring herself to break the news to Gary Rafaloski. Her dad did the job, and Rafaloski was not happy. He felt that *he* could have taken Mary Lou all the way to the Olympics. He resented losing his star pupil when he had brought her so far and she was so close to greatness.

But Mary Lou and her parents had made up their minds. Nobody will ever know how much she could have achieved with Gary Rafaloski as her coach.

The Rettons borrowed a neighbor's station wagon and drove twenty-four hours to Houston. They had arranged for Mary Lou to live with Paige Spiller, another Karolyi gymnast, and her family. She would attend a private school near the gym.

Mary Lou was fourteen. She was in a strange city, with a coach she didn't know, and she had a year to prepare for the Olympics.

She wanted a coach with a forceful personality, and that's what she got. Bela Karolyi was a perfectionist. He was not opposed to yelling and insulting his gymnasts to get them motivated. He worked his girls hard, training most of the day, every day.

At the time, school was of little importance to her. (Mary Lou would drop out after freshman year, and wouldn't graduate until years later.) She had no time for her favorite soap operas, *Guiding Light* and *All My Children*.

At the end of every day she was wiped out, and slept like a rock. One night a tornado swept through Houston and dropped a tree right on the Spillers' house. Mary Lou slept right through it. Mr. Spiller had to pick her up while she was sleeping and carry her to safety.

Karolyi's nickname for Mary Lou was "booboolina," which means "fat." At 4'9" and 100 pounds, she wasn't a skinny little waif, like most gymnasts. She didn't have long, thin lines. Mary Lou was built like a little fullback. Karolyi put her on a diet to bring her down to 94 pounds.

Most girls, it would seem, would feel angered and humiliated by a coach like Bela Karolyi. But Mary Lou thrived on his rough-edged criticism. She and Bela had similar personalities. They were both very outgoing, open, and enthusiastic.

Karolyi liked Retton's style. She was nervy, aggressive, and self-confident. Fearlessly, she would attack the apparatus, running toward the vaulting horse like she was going to knock it over. Pressure only made her perform better.

Just before the McDonald's American Cup in Madison Square Garden, one of America's top gymnasts, Dianne Durham, got hurt and had to pull out. Mary Lou, still an unknown in international competition, was entered as a "walk on."

When the (chalk) dust had settled, she had won the vault and the floor exercise, tied for uneven bars, and won the all-around championship.

Next she was entered into the prestigious Chunici Cup competition in Japan, where she won the vault and the all-around. Very suddenly, Mary Lou Retton was America's top female gymnast and one of the best in the world. At sixteen, she was on the threshold of Olympic greatness.

And no American woman had *ever* won an Olympic medal in gymnastics.

Mary Lou invented two tricks that no other gymnast in the world could do. In the "Retton Vault," she would launch into a lay-out somersault with a full twist and then do a *second* twist.

In the "Retton Flip" on the uneven bars, she would do a handstand on the high bar, then swoop down and slam her belly into the low bar, bounce off it, do a front somersault in the air, and land *sitting* on the high bar with her hands in the air. *Incredible.*

Six weeks before the opening ceremonies, Mary Lou was signing autographs after an exhibition when she felt something funny in her knee. Gymnasts get funny feelings in various parts of their bodies all the time, but this was different.

The knee seized up. Mary Lou could hardly walk, much less run, jump, and land.

Doctors examined the leg and found that cartilage was lodged in the knee socket. They would have to operate. Mary Lou could forget about the Olympics. It would be impossible to heal and get in shape so quickly.

Telling Mary Lou Retton to forget about the Olympics was like telling Picasso to forget about painting or Beethoven to forget about music. Two days after her surgery, she was back in the gym.

She began working out again. Carefully, very carefully. In six weeks, just in time for the opening ceremonies, her knee was completely healed.

The 1984 Olympics were held in Los Angeles, on the UCLA campus. There were many great gymnasts there, but experts predicted the overall championship would come down to Mary Lou Retton and the top Romanian girl, Ecaterina Szabo.

Szabo was another discovery of Bela Karolyi's, from the days he was still in Romania. He was on a hunting trip and one of the men asked him to take a look at his brother's five-year-old daughter. The girl was trotted out and instructed to stand on her head, which she did.

The hunter asked Karolyi to coach the girl at his school. Karolyi refused, explaining that the children had to be at least six years old. He thought that would be the end of it.

But one day, the girl showed up at the school with her father. Karolyi wasn't sure how to handle it, so he went to ask his wife. When they returned, the father was gone and the girl was sitting there sobbing. Her dad had left her there!

Karolyi let the girl hang around the gym, and it turned out she could do more than stand on her head. By seven, she was doing elite compulsory exercises. At twelve, she was the European Junior Champion. She won a silver medal at the 1983 World Championships. And in 1984, Ecaterina Szabo was a favorite to win the Olympics.

Mary Lou, naturally, had home field advantage in Los Angeles. A banner hung high in the Pauley Pavilion read, "WE'RE BETTIN' ON RETTON!"

The two Karolyi protégées battled it out like boxers in a ring. Ecaterina slipped in her bars routine and Retton jumped to a .15 lead. Ecaterina nailed a perfect ten on the beam and Retton scored 9.85 on bars. They were tied.

Ecaterina had the floor exercise next. She wanted to win over the American audience, and she flung her body around the mat to the tunes of *Dixie* and *The Battle Hymn of the Republic*. The judges were impressed and gave her a 9.95 for the effort.

Retton had the balance beam next. The beam was always her weakest event, but she put on one of her best performances ever. It was good enough for a 9.8. Now it was Mary Lou who was .15 behind.

There were two events left, and Mary Lou figured she would need two tens to win the all-around championship. It was next to impossible.

"You have to work now," Bela Karolyi shouted to her, "like you have never worked in your life."

Ecaterina took her turn on the vault. She did a good one, but her legs opened slightly and the judges took off a tiny deduction. The score was 9.9.

Now it was Mary Lou's turn to do her floor exercise. She had chosen a 1930s song titled "Johnny, My Friend."

"Don't hold back," Karolyi urged her. "Go for it. You have nothing to lose."

Mary Lou danced and pranced like a Super Ball. When she was finished, she threw both hands up in the air and leaped into a Karolyi bear hug.

While waiting for the score to come up, Jack Whitaker of ABC television told the worldwide audience, "If she were a tourist attraction, she'd be Niagara Falls."

The scoreboard flashed the score—10.0. By now, the crowd in the Pauley Pavilion was screaming, "U-S-A! U-S-A!"

The floor exercise was not Mary Lou Retton's best event, but she still won the bronze medal at the 1984 Olympics.

Ecaterina's lead was now .05. The championship would come down to her uneven bars routine against Mary Lou's vault.

The bars were not Ecaterina's strongest event, but she was still one of the best in the world. She made a momentary hesitation in the middle of the routine and took a big step back after her dismount from a double somersault. The judges gave her a 9.9.

Everybody started doing arithmetic frantically. If Mary Lou scored a 9.9 on her vault, she would lose. A 9.95 would tie Ecaterina for the gold medal. The only way for Mary Lou to win it for herself would be to nail a 10.0. A perfect ten.

How's that for pressure on a sixteen-year-old girl from West Virginia?

"Here is the vault of your life," Karolyi said, taking Mary Lou by the shoulders. "Be strong and aggressive. Don't hold anything back. Now or never. Stick it!"

After nine years of training, the next four seconds would define the rest of Mary Lou Retton's life. As she walked to the runway, she stepped in a puddle of soda. It didn't bother her. She was focused on the vaulting horse 73.5 feet away.

Jogging in place, she spat on her hands and rubbed them together. The green light, which signaled gymnasts that they could begin, lit up.

The crowd hushed. The only sound in the Pauley Pavilion was the frantic clicking of photographers' shutters.

Mary Lou peered at the horse, glanced down at her takeoff spot, and started sprinting. Arms pumping, she hit the springboard cleanly, flew through the air to the horse, and punched her arms against it.

Her body rocketed upward, legs perfectly together. It was a layout Tsukahara with a twist, and Mary Lou knew the Tsukahara like the rest of us know how to flip on a light switch.

Flying with her ankles over her shoulders, she already knew she'd nailed it. She landed like an arrow in the target.

Mary Lou didn't wait to see the 10.0 come up on the scoreboard. Her arms shot up, and she dashed out to the middle of the floor, waving and smiling. She had defeated Szabo in all-around by the narrowest of margins—.05.

"Winner of the gold medal, scoring seventy-nine point one seven five, representing the United States of America . . . Mary Lou Retton!"

This would be Mary Lou Retton's Olympics. She also won the bronze medal for floor exercise, bronze for uneven bars, silver for the vault, and a silver for the team competition.

After her thrilling triumph, Mary Lou Retton became the first gymnast to *really* cash in on her fame. She gave endorsements for Vidal Sassoon, McDonald's, Hanes, and Holly Farms. She had her own line of clothing. She appeared as herself in the movie *Naked Gun 33⅓*. She did TV commentary and traveled the country giving motivational speeches. She became the first female to appear on a Wheaties box. She was a millionaire before she was old enough to sign her own contracts.

Mary Lou retired from competitive gymnastics in 1986. After getting her high school diploma, she went to the University of Texas. There she met Shannon Kelley, the quarterback of the UT football team. They married in 1990.

In 1995 Mary Lou Retton gave birth to a baby girl named Shayla Rae. The family lives in Houston.

BELA KAROLYI

"A gymnastics meet is like a hunt, in a way. It's you against them. To win, first you make your girls strong. Then they'll jump higher. Work them hard and they'll perform better."

Bela Karolyi can't do a triple back flip off the high bar. If the truth be known, a simple forward roll makes him nauseous. He tried the pommel horse once, and broke his arm.

But because he helped bring both Nadia Comaneci and Mary Lou Retton to greatness, Bela Karolyi is one of the most important figures in gymnastics.

Karolyi was born in 1942 in Transylvania, Romania—the home of Vlad Dracula, better known as Count Dracula. Many people think that is not entirely a coincidence.

As a boy, Bela loved sports, and at one time he owned the Romanian national record for the hammer throw. His father disapproved of athletics. He wanted Bela to be a scientist.

When Bela came home from his high school graduation, his father informed him that he would be going to an interview for engineering school the next day.

"I cannot be there," Bela said. "I have a track meet."

His dad's reaction was to throw him out of the house.

Bela went to Bucharest, the capital of Romania, and enrolled in the University of Physical Education. He enjoyed learning every sport except one—gymnastics. He found that he was terrible at the sport and flunked the gymnastics course.

There was one *good* thing about gymnastics, however. He met Marta Eross, a pretty gymnast. The two fell in love and got married in 1963. Marta helped Bela appreciate the beauty of gymnastics, and the pair began coaching together. They're still at it today.

Together, Bela and Marta developed a new form of gymnastics, which they called "physical gymnastics." Bela had students doing things gymnasts had never done before—lifting weights, running, climbing ropes.

The Karolyi idea was that gymnasts should be not just technically and artistically beautiful, but also dynamic, powerful, aggressive, and daring. The way to achieve that was by endless repetition and non-stop training.

When Nadia Comaneci shocked the world at the 1976 Olympics, the gymnastic world saw that the Karolyi system worked. And when Mary Lou Retton did the same in 1984, Bela's place in gymnastics history was assured.

Controversy seems to follow Bela. He is outspoken. He doesn't care what people think of him. He has no patience for people—gymnasts, judges, authorities—who anger him. He makes enemies easily.

During the 1980 Olympics in Moscow, he became infuriated at the judging, so he knocked the scoreboard down and led his team out during the awards ceremony.

Karolyi's hotheaded temperament didn't fit comfortably with the Communist system before the end of the Cold War. He found that he was constantly watched and followed. His home and his phone were bugged. He feared he would be imprisoned by government officials he had offended.

It was Marta who suggested they defect to the West.

The date was March 30, 1981. They were in a New York City hotel on the final day of an exhibition tour with the Romanian team. Bela and Marta realized how easy it would be to walk out of the hotel in the middle of the night and request political asylum in America.

There was just one problem—the Karolyi's six-year-old daughter, Andrea, was back in Romania, waiting for them to come home.

Bela and Marta stayed up all night talking things over. Finally they came to a decision. They would *not* get on the plane home. They would try to make a go of it in America. They would send for Andrea as soon as they could. In the meantime, she would be safe with relatives.

Before he walked out the door, Bela had to say good-bye to his star pupil, Nadia Comaneci. He pulled her aside and whispered the news.

"I don't want to go back either," she said, crying. "Let me stay with you."

Bela was afraid that if Nadia joined him, it would appear as though he had kidnapped her. He urged her to go home and finish college.*

At 3:00 that morning, Bela and Marta walked into the streets of New York with two suitcases and a big stuffed bear they were planning to bring home to Andrea. They didn't even have money to catch a taxicab. For a few nights they would stay with Marta's aunt, who had come to the U.S. in 1938.

The Karolyis found their way to Long Beach, California, where they rented a hotel room for seven dollars a night. Bela got part time jobs—loading freight on ships, sweeping restaurant floors. He made very little money. Some days, Bela and Marta would share a single pretzel as their three meals.

* She did. In 1989, the same year Bela Karolyi was granted American citizenship, Nadia defected.

The couple learned English by watching soap operas and *Sesame Street*.

Back home, the Romanian government had confiscated everything in the Karolyi house. Bela and Marta had to wait a month before they could speak to Andrea by telephone. It would be nearly a year before she was allowed to join her parents in America.

Gradually, Bela connected with people he had met in the gymnastics community. Coaching jobs were offered to him, and he gratefully accepted.

In 1983, some investors approached Bela about starting a gym in Houston. He jumped at the chance, and as soon as he could afford to, bought the investors out so he could own the gym himself.

Back then, many people believed that Americans had never been very good at gymnastics because American kids are spoiled. They have it too easy. They only want to have fun. They're not willing to give up video games, dances, and movies to sweat in a gym all day so they can reach the top.

Karolyi believed kids are the same all over the world. He went around Houston tacking posters for his gym up on trees. When he took over the gym, he had 86 students. By the end of 1983 he had 250. Young gymnasts from all over the country, it turned out, wanted to be coached by the man who had made a star of Nadia Comaneci.

One of these was Mary Lou Retton. And after her success, Karolyi had 1,400 students.

Today, the Karolyi complex in Houston includes a gym, dormitories, a swimming pool, tennis courts, and a ranch populated by goats, deer, horses, pheasants, camels, llamas, donkeys, chickens, turkeys, raccoons, pigeons, pigs, beagles, and cattle.

———

At the beginning of this section, Bela Karolyi was compared with Dracula. Some people might prefer Dr. Frankenstein. Karolyi, his critics contend, takes girls who are too young and pushes them too hard.

The Karolyi gym is sometimes referred to as The Factory, because gymnasts are mass-produced there. The girls work out eight hours a day, close to fifty hours a week. There are no vacations.

Karolyi has been accused of calling his students cruel names, and kicking them out of the gym when they cry about it. He is so strict about weight control that he gets furious when he sees his gymnasts eating. They have to resort to smuggling food into their rooms as though it were something illegal.

Bela Karolyi explains it all to Kim Zmeskal during the 1991 American Cup.

He has been accused of getting angry when gymnasts get hurt, and refusing to give them medical attention. If a girl doesn't perform up to his standards, he has been known to make her *teammates* do extra work.

This is how Karolyi narrows down the field to the toughest, most ambitious, and most talented gymnasts.

"He seeks reckless kids," according to *Sports Illustrated*, "unsophisticated girls who can be molded into superior gymnasts who do what they're told and don't cry."

Love him or hate him (there doesn't seem to be any in-between), Bela Karolyi has achieved results. Despite all the criticism, many of the best gymnasts in the world continue to flock to him.

In 1996 he is leading former champions Kim Zmeskal, Svetlana Boginskaya and thirteen-year-old sensation Dominique Moceanu to the Olympics.

THE UNSUNG SUPERSTARS

Most people probably think Olga Korbut, Nadia Comaneci, and Mary Lou Retton completely dominated the other gymnasts when they became worldwide sensations. Actually, they didn't.

When Olga Korbut was getting all the attention at the 1972 Olympic Games, Karin Janz of Germany won gold medals for the vault and uneven bars. The all-around gold medal was won by Olga's teammate Ludmilla Tourischeva. Olga came in seventh.

When everyone was astonished by Nadia Comaneci in the 1976 Olympics, Nelli Kim of the Soviet Union scored two perfect 10.0s herself and won gold medals for floor exercise and vaulting. Now, to people outside the sport, she's a trivia question, and a tough one at that.

In 1984, Mary Lou Retton won just one gold medal (of eighty-three golds won by the United States). The woman she beat by .05, Ecaterina Szabo, won gold medals for vault, floor exercise, and balance beam. Mary Lou's teammate Julianne McNamara won the gold on the uneven bars and also became the first American woman to score a 10.0.

But Olga, Nadia, and Mary Lou are the ones people remember. Something about these three young women captured the world's imagination—Olga's emotional ups and downs, Nadia's sheer artistic brilliance, and Mary Lou's uninhibited enthusiasm.

There have been many gymnasts who put on incredible Olympic performances but never got the cheers they deserved. Here are a few of them:

• Viktor Chukarin (Soviet Union): He spent four years in a concentration camp during World War II. He survived it, and in the 1952 Olympics won two gold medals and two silvers. He became a schoolteacher between Olympics, but came back in 1956 to win three golds, a silver, and a bronze.

• Sawao Kato (Japan): Just 5'3", he won the all-around championships in the 1968 and 1972 Olympics. Injuries kept him out of the 1974 World Championships, and it looked like he was through. Then he came back and at age twenty-nine won another gold on the parallel bars in the 1976 Olympics. Sawao won eight golds, three silvers, and one bronze altogether.

• Nikolai Andrianov (Soviet Union): He was called "Old One Leg" by coaches because his legs were always perfectly together. In the 1972, 1976, and 1980 Olympics he won a total of fifteen medals, including seven golds. He was the first to do a triple back somersault off the high bar in international competition.

• Aleksandr Ditiatin (Soviet Union): His father took him to a gym when he was eight because Aleksandr was stoop-shouldered. It must have helped. In 1980, he became the first person to win eight medals in one Olympics. He was also the first male gymnast to receive a ten in the Olympics, on the vault.

• Larissa Latynina (Soviet Union): Her father died in World War II and her mother died when she was very young. Larissa didn't perform particularly difficult moves and she wasn't an innovator, but everything she did, she did *perfectly*. Among the 1956, 1960, and 1964 Olympics she carried home eighteen medals, at least one on every event, nine of them golds. Within those years she also gave birth to two children.

• Vera Čáslavská (Czechoslovakia): A former figure skater,

Vera Čáslavská was one of the first great women gymnasts. In the 1964 and 1968 Olympics, she won 18 medals, 7 of them gold.

Čáslavská saw Czech gymnastics champion Eva Bosakova on television inviting young women to come see a competition. She took up gymnastics and won eighteen medals. Between the 1964 and 1968 Olympics, Čáslavská won seven golds.

She was quite famous in her day. Čáslavská once mentioned in an interview that her hobby was collecting postcards. Three days later she received 3,500 of them.

3

The Events

In the game of football, one player throws the ball (the quarterback). Another catches the ball (receiver). Somebody else runs with the ball (fullback). And they keep a fourth guy around simply to kick an occasional field goal. The athletes have to do only one thing really well—and that's the way it is in many sports.

But to reach the top in gymnastics, an athlete has to be good at *everything*.

The events are so different. Long arms are a big advantage for the pommel horse, but it's good to have short arms on the rings. Strong muscles are important for all the events (particularly the rings), but flexibility and balance are much more important on the balance beam.

It's a very rare athlete who is versatile enough to be an all-around gymnastics champion.

The apparatus is primitive and simple. The horizontal bar is like a tree limb. The beam is like a tightrope. The pommel horse is like, well, a horse. What's interesting is how ingenious and daring human beings can be on these simple pieces of equipment.

In this chapter, we're going to look at the gymnastic events one by one. There are four events for women, and six for men.

Women	*Men*
Uneven Bars	Parallel Bars
Vault	Horizontal Bar
Balance Beam	Vault
Floor Exercise	Floor Exercise
	Pommel Horse
	Rings

PARALLEL BARS (FOR MEN ONLY)

The apparatus: The bars are 67 inches off the floor and 11.5 feet long. They can be adjusted from 17 to 19 inches apart, and also up and down (for young gymnasts). They used to be made of wood, but are now made of fiberglass with a wood coating. The bars have a little bounce to them.

"P-Bars," as they are often called, were invented by Frederick Jahn in 1812 because he believed that young Germans didn't have enough arm strength.

Back then, gymnasts performed very slowly on the bars, using brute strength to hold very difficult positions. Now, parallel bar routines include a lot of swinging, somersaulting, and soaring above and below the bars, with a few strength moves.

In almost every routine, the gymnast will swing his legs up for a handstand and freeze it up there. He is required to be stationary for two to three seconds to get credit for a "hold" move.

The gymnast will receive extra credit if he performs moves using

Huang Lipsing of China. Don't try this on your banister at home.

just one bar. Watch for a flying backward somersault, and a "Stütz," when he swings his legs forward and upward, releases one hand, turns his body, releases the other hand, and then grasps both bars again facing in the opposite direction.

A parallel bars routine must include at least one release move—a move in which both hands leave the bars and then regrasp them. It must also have a move performed below the bars.

Watch to see if the gymnast's body is straight, with arms locked and shoulders aligned over his hands. This event requires great balance. Small gymnasts with powerful shoulders have an advantage.

Routines usually last about 25 to 30 seconds, with no time limit.

HORIZONTAL BAR (FOR MEN ONLY)

The apparatus: The bar is 94.5 inches long and about 100 inches above the ground. It is made of spring steel about an inch thick. Mats fill the floor below.

The horizontal bar (or high bar) requires strong arms, hands, and fingers, as well as a large dose of courage.

Mostly, you will see the gymnast doing big swinging circles around the bar. Forward ones, backward ones, straight ones, bent ones, and straddled ones.

A "giant" swing is a move in which the gymnast swings all the way around the bar with his arms and legs completely straight. The pull on his shoulders at the bottom of a giant can be five times the force of gravity. And sometimes gymnasts do it with one hand!

High bar routines last 25 to 30 seconds, with no time limit. The gymnast must do twists, changes of grip, and at least one release move. He cannot stop in the middle of his routine.

If you watch the gymnast's hands, you will notice that sometimes he grasps the bar with his palms facing down (overgrasp), and other times his palms will be facing up (undergrasp). The direction of grip is important. To avoid losing his grip and falling off the bar, he must point his thumbs in the direction he's moving. When he swings forward, his thumbs point away from him. When he swings back, his thumbs face back.

The high bar is considered the most spectacular men's event, and it can be frightening for some people just to *watch*. The guy may be as high as fourteen feet off the ground, upside down, and moving very fast. If his hand slips, he's going to fly a long way. Crash landings are not pretty.

The high bar is usually the final event. That makes it even more tense, because the gymnast may need to achieve a certain score to win the competition, and everybody knows it.

UNEVEN BARS (FOR WOMEN ONLY)

The apparatus: The uneven bars are a cross between the parallel bars and high bar. The bars are 94.5 inches long. The higher bar is 7.5 feet off the ground, the lower one about 5 feet. The two bars are 5 to 6 feet apart. They are adjustable in height and distance from one another. They are made of fiberglass with a wood covering, and have a good bounce.

Svetlana Boginskaya soars over the uneven bars. She has won three Olympic gold medals.

The uneven bars is the most recent event in gymnastics. It was first demonstrated at the 1936 Olympics, and became a part of the competition in 1952.

Women used to practice on the men's parallel bars, until some-one—nobody knows who—thought of making one bar high and the other one lower. This enabled the women gymnasts to create routines that were based on grace and flexibility more than strength.

At first the women didn't swing much on the bars. They did a lot of balletic poses. Now they do tricks like the ones the men do on the high bar—release moves, twists, somersaults, hand changes, changes of direction, pirouettes.

In the 1960s, gymnasts were allowed to stop twice in the middle of a routine. In the 1970s, they could stop once. Now they're not allowed to stop at all. They must keep a continuous flowing action with at least ten movements linked together.

Both bars have to be used, and the gymnast is allowed no more than five moves in a row on one bar. She is required to change hand holds, change directions, and have at least two "flight elements" in her routine.

A routine lasts about 30 seconds. The gymnast will dismount with somersaults or twists in the air. She will be judged on her form, her hand grips, the way her body passed between the bars, and how difficult her tricks were.

Timing is crucial on the uneven bars. If the gymnast doesn't launch every trick perfectly, she will have to make midair corrections. If she leaps for a bar and finds herself a few inches too close to it, she can make a slight change in her body to fix things. Maybe the judges won't notice. But if she's a few inches too far away from the bar, all she can do is hope there's a soft mat underneath.

Falling in this event can be dangerous. A girl can crack her head on the lower bar.

The uneven bars requires strength, grace, and agility. It was on this event that Nadia Comaneci scored the first perfect 10.0 in Olympic history.

RIPS AND GRIPS: THE GYMNAST'S HANDS

"I can't wear rings," American gymnast Cathy Rigby once said, "because my hands are so ugly."

Gymnastics is tough on an athlete's ankles, knees, back, and shoulders, but the body part that really takes a beating on a daily basis is the hands. Swinging on the high bar, parallel bars, or uneven bars puts a tremendous amount of friction on the palms, even though a bars routine lasts less than a minute.

"Even if you had the strength and endurance to stay up there longer than a minute, you couldn't, because your hands would burn up," says United States Olympic coach Don Peters.

There are a few things gymnasts can do to care for their hands. They rub pumice stone on them to prevent calluses from building up. Mary Lou Retton used to put Vaseline and vitamin E on her hands at night, and then wear socks on her hands as she slept.

When they're on the bars and rings, gymnasts wear a handguard or "grip"—a leather strap that fits over the fingers and fastens at the wrist. The grip reduces friction and protects the palms from blisters.

Starting in the mid-1970s, horizontal bar artists began using grips with a dowel sewn into them. This enabled them to hold onto the bar tighter and do more spectacular moves.

The one thing all gymnasts do before getting on the bars is "chalk up." They dip their hands (and often their feet) into a large bowl of powdered chalk that absorbs moisture and reduces friction. The chalk—sometimes called "mag"—is made from magnesium carbonate and calcium carbonate (the same stuff blackboard chalk is made from).

They have to be careful not to put too much chalk on, because the loose chalk can fall in their eyes while they're swinging upside down.

Gymnasts use so much chalk that there is often a haze of chalk dust hanging in the air in a gym. Some people have worried that it may be harmful to breathe under these conditions. But studies have found no evidence that breathing small amounts of chalk dust is hazardous to health. The mouth, nose, and lungs do a good job of filtering it out.

No matter what they do to protect their hands, all gymnasts sometimes get "rips"—a tearing of the skin in which the outer layer separates from lower layers. Rips are common, and painful. A gymnast just has to hope it doesn't happen the day before a major competition.

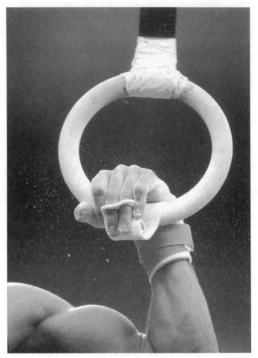

Grips reduce friction on the hands and make many of today's spectacular tricks on the bars and rings possible.

VAULT (FOR MEN AND WOMEN)

The apparatus: The "horse" is made from moisture absorbent suede or leather and padded to ease the stress on the gymnast's wrists and shoulders. It's about 47 inches tall for women, a little higher for men. The runway leading up to the horse is 82 feet.

The vault is the only event that consists of a single skill, but it's a very complicated skill that consists of four different parts:
• Run-up: This is probably the most important part of the vault, because if the run-up isn't strong, the whole vault will be ruined. Top gymnasts will reach 17 m.p.h. on their way to the horse.

"If you want to be a good vaulter," Mary Lou Retton advised a reader in *USA Gymnastics*, "you can't slow down when you're running to the board. Don't be afraid. Just make sure your steps are right and go for it."

Gymnasts take the same number of strides to the horse each time they vault, and each gymnast's number may be different. Retton's run was always 73.5 feet.

If they find themselves out of sync on the run-up, the women are allowed to veer off before touching the horse and start again. The men don't get that second chance.

• Preflight: On the ground in front of the horse is a "Reuther board" (designed by a German man named Richard Reuther). It's about 2 feet by 4 feet, and has thick springs inside. At the end of her run, the gymnast will leap off this springboard with both feet and launch herself headfirst toward the horse. The better the vaulter,

This gymnast is about to "punch" the horse with 500 pounds of pressure to rocket herself as high and as far as possible.

the farther the board is placed from the horse.

It's tricky. If she leans too far forward, she won't press down on the board enough to get a good push-off. If she's leaning too far backward, she'll lose speed and get pushed *up* instead of forward. She doesn't want to get too much height here, because that will cost speed and power. But let's assume she flies to the horse correctly.

• Afterflight: Using her hands, the vaulter will push off or "punch" the horse with 500 pounds of pressure per square inch. She wants to get as high as possible here, because the longer she's in the air, the more she can do with her body. Top vaulters will get 8 feet off the ground.

Years ago, it was considered difficult for gymnasts to do a handspring or somersault off the horse. Then they started doing them with a twist of the body or a piked position. Now you'll see vaulters do multiple twists and flips in the air with their bodies perfectly straight. It's pretty incredible.

One thing you *won't* see are vaults in a cartwheel position. They were found to cause a lot of knee injuries upon landing, and are no longer allowed in competition.

• Landing: Imagine—gymnasts can dash 17 MPH, rocket themselves into the air, and then land without taking a step on the mat. It requires perfect execution and hundreds of practice vaults to do this perfectly.

The shock of the landing is absorbed by the hips, ankles, and knees. The vaulter can bend her knees a little, but if she bends them too much her score will be lowered.

Finally, she raises both hands triumphantly (and to help balance herself). The whole event takes about five seconds.

Vaults are scored for height, distance, body position, landing, and degree of difficulty. A vaulter's legs have to be straight and together, with the toes pointed. The more twists and flips in the air, the higher the score.

Women vault across the side of the horse, while the men leap over its length.

There are dozens of different vaults. The Japanese have been innovators in this event, and the two most popular vaults are named after their inventors, Haruhiru Yamashita and Mitsuo Tsukahara. The first one-arm vault was performed by Grant Carlyon in 1985 at the Australian Games.

HAPPY LANDINGS

The one thing casual fans who can't tell a perfect Tsukahara from a rotten Yurchenko can all see and understand is the gymnast's dismount. This ending to the routine is also the last thing the judges see, and it may leave a strong impression.

Even people who know nothing about gymnastics can tell if a landing is a good one. If the gymnast hits the mat like a knife stuck in the earth, she's done it perfectly. If she takes a step upon landing, that's good, but not great. And if she falls down, well, that's awful.

The top gymnasts are so close in ability, first place decisions often come down to who took that tiny step after landing and who didn't.

Gymnasts call a perfect landing "sticking." "I've gotta stick this dismount," she might say to herself. "I stuck it!"

Sticking a dismount requires perfect timing on the takeoff. A fraction of a second too early, and you land on your face. Too late, and you break your neck.

The dismount also requires good form, good "air sense," and powerful quadriceps (thigh muscles). And a lot of practice. Gymnasts usually learn to dismount by jumping into a swimming-pool-sized pit filled with foam.

The gymnast will try to land balanced, her arms extended in front and out to the sides a bit. Her feet should be a few inches apart and turned out slightly to make a solid base. She should bend her legs slightly to absorb the impact. Then she should give a little wave to the crowd and wait for the score to come up.

BALANCE BEAM (FOR WOMEN ONLY)

The apparatus: The beam is about 16 feet long, 4 feet off the ground, and 4 inches wide. It is made of laminated wood covered with chamois. The height can be adjusted.

In Uzbekistan, a small country in what used to be the Soviet Union, the national pastime is tightrope walking. Every town has a group of rope walkers, and national championships are held every year. The sport was invented there, legend has it, by Mohammed's brother Ali, who led his men in battle across a rope lassoed to an enemy fortress.

The balance beam is the gymnastic equivalent of the tightrope. For people who aren't gymnasts, just *walking a straight line* on a

4-inch beam 4 feet off the ground is hard to do. Forget about somersaults, splits, handsprings, walkovers, cartwheels, backflips, and backward rolls. Most gymnasts consider the balance beam the most difficult event.

"Everyone is scared on the beam," Canadian coach Boris Bajin once told *Sports Illustrated*. "No matter how good they are, they are all shaking inside." The Germans call it *Angst Baum*—"fear beam."

The balance beam isn't as physically demanding as the other events. But it demands perfect balance, intense concentration, and years of practice.

A balance beam routine looks a lot like a floor exercise. In fact, a novice "beamer" starts by performing along a 4-inch-wide line on the floor. Once she masters that, she tries to do the same thing on a beam a few inches off the floor. As she develops skill and confidence, the beam will be raised gradually.

The difference between walking the beam and doing a floor exercise is that the beam must be walked much more *precisely*. On the floor, the gymnast can keep her hands and feet at shoulder width for balance. When they're in contact with the beam, her hands or feet must stay together. The rest of her body has to be in perfect alignment.

Just getting *on* the beam is hard. Some gymnasts walk onto it, others run, and still others use a springboard. Daring gymnasts will do a difficult mount so they can pile up points early. Others play it safe, make sure they get on cleanly, and go for a more challenging dismount. There are dozens of ways to mount and dismount the beam.

A routine must last 70 to 90 seconds. The gymnast must use the entire length of the beam, and you will usually see her cover that distance at least six times.

Most gymnasts consider the balance beam to be the toughest event. Here, Mo Huilan of China competes in the 1994 World Championships.

The judges don't like it when a gymnast takes a deep breath and pauses before attempting a difficult move. They want to see a continuous, flowing program. One movement should go right into the next one.

Two "flight elements" are required, and the gymnasts will sometimes get 3 or 4 feet above the beam. Getting that high actually makes landing *easier* because it gives the gymnast more time to get her foot back where it should be to land on the beam. If she takes just a little hop, there's no time to make a correction on the way down.

When Olga Korbut did the first back somersault on the beam in the 1972 Olympics, everybody's jaws dropped open. People had assumed that such a stunt was impossible. Today, it's impossible for a gymnast to reach the top unless she can do a back somersault.

There are a few little tricks a gymnast uses to make the beam seem a little wider. When she grasps the beam with her hands, she'll lay her palms flat on the top surface and wrap her fingers down the sides. When walking the beam, she swivels her feet left and right slightly to use the entire surface.

The balance beam is the most unforgiving of all the events. On the other apparatus, the gymnast can make a tiny mistake and compensate for it in some way. Sometimes the judges won't even notice. Tiny mistakes are more costly on the beam—you fall off!

FLOOR EXERCISE (FOR MEN AND WOMEN)

The apparatus: There are no bars, pommels, or rings to help or hurt the gymnast. The floor *is* the apparatus. This is a battle between a human being and gravity. "People think the floor exercise is the safest thing we do," says Kurt Thomas, "but it's not true. You've got nothing to hold on to out there but air."

As recently as the mid-1960s, floor exercises were performed on a plain wooden floor or on canvas stretched over the floor. This was very dangerous, and gymnasts could not perform the daring tricks they do today. Now they perform on a "floating floor"—plywood covered by 2-inch padding and mounted on 4-inch springs or foam blocks. The area is 12 meters square, which is almost 40 feet square.

The floor exercise—a combination of ballet, modern dance, and tumbling—didn't become a part of the Olympics until 1932.

In 70 to 90 seconds (50 to 70 seconds for men), spectators will most often see four tumbling runs. These are when the gymnast dashes across the floor and performs a series of handsprings, somersaults, and other tricks. She will probably do her most difficult "pass" first, when she has the most energy.

Watch her legs. They tell how difficult the move is. If her legs are tucked against her chin, that's easiest. If they are piked (straight, with a bend at the waist) that's harder. And if the whole body is straight, that's the hardest of all. It's called a layout.

The top gymnasts defy gravity—double back somersaults, double *twisting* somersaults. Kim Zmeskal would do the "triple whip back"—three consecutive back flips in which the hands never touch the floor. Valeri Liukin would do triple back somersaults. It

Eleven-year-old Jennie Thompson of the U.S. tied for first place on "floor" at the 1992 Junior National Championships—making her the youngest champion for this event in history.

doesn't look humanly possible. They resemble mechanical wind-up toys.

The gymnasts will link these tumbling passes together by doing "transitions" in the corners of the floor. Look for the "Y-scale," when the gymnast (usually male) stands on one foot and brings the other leg all the way up to his head without bending it.

The men will get down on the floor and do pommel horse moves, flinging their legs around. The top male gymnasts can actually lie face down on the floor and slowly raise their bodies up with the hands into a full handstand.

The women's floor exercise is the only event done with musical accompaniment. The judges look for grace, balance, flexibility, and emotional expression in the women.

Floor exercise used to feature a lot more dance, but in recent years the focus has been more on athletics. "If they wanted to see dancing," says Mary Lou Retton, "they'd go to the ballet."

You won't see the men dance or express emotion. They're expected to perform explosive acrobatics and stronger movements with higher elevation. Their somersaults are done at shoulder height, or even higher.

POMMEL HORSE (FOR MEN ONLY)

The apparatus: The pommel horse is basically a vaulting horse with two adjustable 4-inch-high U-shaped wooden handles—pommels—about 1 foot, 5 inches apart. The two ends of the horse used to be called the "neck" and the "croup," and the center section the "saddle." Nowadays it's right end, middle, and left end. The pommel horse is sometimes called a "side horse."

As discussed in the first chapter, Roman soldiers used a primitive horse to practice mounting and dismounting their real horses. But the pommel horse, like the vault, goes back to 3000 B.C. In Minoan Crete, the men did something called "bull-leaping." They would leap on a stampeding bull, grab the horns, and swing themselves around the bull's head.

And you thought the *pommel horse* looked difficult!

Even without a live animal, the pommel horse is probably the toughest men's event. It's not dangerous like some of the others, but it requires balance, strength, speed, flexibility, and timing. Years of practice are needed to master it.

Peter Vidmar, who won the gold medal in this event at the 1984 Olympics, used to call the pommel horse "the Monster."

A routine lasts 30 to 40 seconds, with no time limit. While supporting his weight entirely with his hands, the gymnast "rides" the horse, swinging his legs over and around it without sitting on it.

His hands have to move very quickly. He has to keep his body's center of gravity above his hands as he moves around the horse. If he bumps a shin slightly, it will throw off his timing or he'll crash to the floor. He cannot let any part of his body except his hands touch the horse.

A standard move is the "double leg circle." With his hands on the pommels, the gymnast swings both legs together in circles around the horse. Legs and toes should be pointed straight at all times. He has to move his hands on each rotation to get them out of the way.

When he does a "scissors," his legs are wide apart and he swings them on either side of the horse like a pendulum. The gymnast who swings his legs highest and farthest is the best, in the eyes of the judges. And he cannot *lift* his legs. He has to swing them.

Using all three sections of the horse, the gymnast wants to keep his hips out, and his body in a perfectly straight line. "You should be like a long stick swinging from the shoulders," says Peter Vidmar.

At some point in his routine, the gymnast has to support himself with his hands behind his back. This requires very strong shoulders, wrists and forearms. Long arms are an advantage in this event, because they keep the body away from the horse.

The pommel horse also requires incredible concentration. Gymnasts report that if they focus on one thing, they tend to forget everything else they need to do. The best strategy on this event is to go into a sort of trance and let muscle memory take over.

You won't see changes in speed on the pommel horse, and you won't see spectacular flipping dismounts. This is the hardest event to make look easy.

The pommel horse is usually the first event in the men's competition, and the gymnast who wins this event will often win the all-around title.

Mihai Bagiu on the pommel horse.

RINGS (FOR MEN ONLY)

The apparatus: The rings are 7 inches in diameter, made of wood or fiberglass, and hang about 100 inches above the mats. Short nylon or leather straps attach the rings to steel cables that stretch to the ceiling or a metal frame.

When this apparatus was invented in the 1800s, instead of rings there were two short bars the gymnast would grab. Later they were triangles. By the turn of the century, they had become the circular rings we see today.

This event, more than any other, requires brute strength. The gymnast's arms, shoulders, chest, and back must be incredibly powerful and flexible at the same time. Because the rings swing freely, the gymnast is forced to devote part of his strength to holding them still. On all the other events, the apparatus stays in one place.

A rings routine lasts 30 to 50 seconds, with no time limit. The gymnast will swing or muscle his body into a series of positions. At least two of these will be handstands. All the strength positions must be held steady for 2 to 3 seconds.

The most familiar strength move is the "Iron Cross." In this move the gymnast's body is upright, and he thrusts his arms straight out from the shoulders with a ring in each hand. It takes an almost unbelievable amount of strength.

You will probably see him perform an "L support" (arms straight down, trunk upright, hips bent so legs are parallel to the floor), a "planche" (entire body parallel to the floor, above the rings, face down) and the painful sounding "dislocate" (swing backward through an upside-down hang to a right-side-up long hang while rotating his shoulders).

Through all these positions, the gymnast attempts to keep the rings motionless. His arms and legs should be straight for almost all the moves, his body stiff as a board. His muscles shouldn't quiver. His eyes shouldn't bulge out of their sockets. Swings should be smooth, not jerky. Points are deducted if his arms touch the straps. Gymnasts who have short arms are at an advantage in this event.

The lords of the rings, of course, make it all look easy.

A gymnast spends a lot of time upside down on the rings, and he doesn't want to fall on his head. When learning a new trick, he wears a safety belt around his waist. Ropes extend from the belt up to pulleys. If the gymnast is about to fall, his coach or fellow gymnast can yank the rope and prevent him from hitting the ground. Instead, he hangs a few feet off the floor, like a marionette.

The "iron cross" demands incredible strength. Even the best gymnasts in the world can only hold this move about seven seconds.

THE ROLE OF THE COACH

If gymnastic tricks look dangerous, they *are*. But the best gymnasts minimize the danger by practicing each move hundreds of times under the watchful eye of a coach. By the time you see her do it on TV, she can practically perform the trick in her sleep. If she botches it, she was probably not ready to perform it in competition.

The first time she does a trick, the gymnast's coach essentially picks her up and physically guides her body through it. Together, they watch videos of the trick being done correctly, and then break the trick down into smaller parts.

While she learns how to do the trick and develops confidence, the coach or "spotter" stands close by, ready to catch her or give her a little shove in the right direction if she needs it. The gymnast has to trust that her coach will be there if she's going to attempt increasingly difficult moves.

"One of the most difficult decisions for a coach," according to Donna Strauss, director of Parkettes in Allentown, Pennsylvania, "is to decide when a gymnast has mastered a skill well enough to perform it by herself."

OTHER FORMS OF GYMNASTICS

Rhythmic Gymnastics

The gymnastics that most people are familiar with is called "artistic gymnastics." Another form of the sport is "rhythmic gymnastics," which is sometimes referred to as *"gymnastique moderne."*

Rhythmic gymnastics is performed *with* the apparatus, not *on* it. The athletes (who are all women) do routines to musical accompaniment using a rope, hoop, ball, club, or ribbon, according to the event. They are not allowed to use gold, silver, or bronze-colored equipment, for obvious reasons.

The gymnast will throw the rope high in the air, do a split-legged leap while waiting for it to come down, and then catch one end in each hand. She'll toss a ball, do a somersault, and catch the ball without missing a beat. She'll throw the hoop, catch it, roll it, spin it, balance it, or jump through it. She'll twirl the clubs around her body and fling them in the air. She'll wave the ribbon around to create arcs, spirals, and complicated patterns. It's a very beautiful sport to watch.

Rhythmic gymnasts create arcs, spirals, and complicated patterns with a long ribbon.

75

Handsprings, aerials and other acrobatics are not allowed in rhythmic gymnastics. That's one reason why the athletes tend to be taller, heavier, and older than artistic gymnasts. Also, they suffer from fewer injuries.

The key to success at rhythmic gymnastics, according to USA Gymnastics (formerly the United States Gymnastics Federation), is "to keep the movement pure and natural, striving to exclude distracting and risky acrobatic elements and to maintain harmony of the body movements with the apparatus." As in all sports, that is more difficult than it looks.

There are two panels of judges in rhythmic gymnastics, one to evaluate what the gymnast does and the other to evaluate how well she does it. As in artistic gymnastics, the athletes can get a maximum score of 10.0. The more difficult the elements in a routine, the higher the score is likely to be.

Rhythmic gymnastics began in the Soviet Union. It's very popular in Eastern Europe, where competitions have been held since the 1920s. In Spain, you can walk into sporting goods stores and buy rhythmic equipment.

The first World Championship was held in Budapest in 1963. Rhythmic became a part of the Olympic Games in 1984, when Canada's Lori Fung won the gold medal. Marina Lobatch of the Soviet Union was the champ at the 1988 Olympics, and Alexandra Timoshenko of the Unified team took the gold in 1992.

In America, few people appreciate rhythmic gymnastics, or even take it seriously as a sport. "In the minds of many, there is no more ridiculous a sport in the Olympics than synchronized swimming, unless it happens to be rhythmic gymnastics," snickered *The New York Times* in 1995.

But then, hardly anybody took *artistic* gymnastics seriously until

Olga Korbut came along. Maybe rhythmic is just waiting for its Olga.

Acrobatics

Imagine a male gymnast on the floor, performing a split. His arms are raised, and handstanding on top of his hands is a female gymnast. Above her and standing on her feet is a ten-year-old girl.

You're likely to see something like this in sports acrobatics, which is sometimes called "tumbling," "adagio," "hand-balancing," "pyramid-building," "acrogymnastics," or simply "acro."

The Greek word "akrobatos" means to climb or to rise. Acrobatics was performed by the ancient Chinese, Greeks, Romans, and Egyptians. Acrobats are a standby of circuses around the world.

As a sport, acrobatic competitions were first held in the Soviet Union in 1939. International competitions began in 1957 in Poland. The International Federation of Sports Acrobats was founded in 1973. The following year they held the first World Championship in Moscow. Eight nations and eighty-eight acrobats participated.

The Russians and Chinese have consistently proven themselves to be the best acrobats in the world.

The United States Sports Acrobatics Federation held its first national championship in 1976. In 1987, the sport was officially recognized by the International Olympic Committee. It is not yet a part of the Olympics.

In competition you'll see women's pairs, men's pairs, mixed pairs, girl's trio, and four men performing at the same time. Routines are accompanied by music, and last about 3 minutes.

Sports acrobatics requires the gymnast to have total trust of the partner, who is, in a way, the apparatus. It's not surprising that fami-

"Acro" is not yet an Olympic sport, but it is one of the most exciting and daring types of gymnastics.

lies have formed acrobatic teams. A few that have gained fame over the years are the Flying Concellos, the Peerless Potters, the Six American Bedfords, the Rubio Sisters, and the Cycling Jacksons.

The most famous acrobats of all were the Great Wallendas. Karl Wallenda was the founder and leader of the troupe. He and his family did a high-wire balancing act that thrilled audiences around the world for years. They successfully performed a seven-man pyramid in 1947.

Sadly, the Wallendas went a little too far in their efforts to astonish audiences. When they were doing the same stunt in 1962, the pyramid collapsed. Two Wallendas were killed and one was paralyzed. Another member of the team was paralyzed in 1963.

In 1978, seventy-three-year-old Karl Wallenda was walking a 120-foot wire in Puerto Rico when a gust of wind blew him off and to his death.

Trampoline

Back in 1936, American diving and tumbling champion George Nissen was looking for a new way to practice when he hit on the idea of creating a cloth springboard that would fling a person up in the air. Nissen built a device in his father's garage in Grand Rapids, Iowa, using scrap metal, springs, and canvas.

He called the new sport "rebound tumbling." Today, the device and the sport are called trampoline. ("Trampolin" is Spanish for springboard and "trampoli" is Italian for performing on stilts, but some people say the trampoline was named after a French acrobat in the Middle Ages.)

Trampoline used to be a popular high-school sport, but these days it is used mostly to teach other gymnastic skills. The main reason the sport has declined is that so many people have been seriously injured on trampolines. A somersault that is timed just a little bit off can throw a person to the ground with his or her entire body weight landing on the head and neck.

The following warning label appears in one gymnastics catalog next to a trampoline: "Death or paralysis can result from improper use of this piece of equipment."

In a Diamidov, the gymnast turns 360 degrees after a swing up to a handstand on the parallel bars. It is named for Sergei Diamidov of the Soviet Union, who invented it. Here, Felix Aguilera of Cuba performs a Diamidov at the 1992 World Championships.

Vitaly Scherbo of Belarus performing a layout full-in, full-out, which is also called a double-double. Scherbo is one of the few gymnasts in the world who can do this.

Oksana Chusovitina of the Uzbekistan performing an inverted giant. This is a move for men on the high bar that women now do on the uneven bars.

Aljaz Pegan of Slovenia was having trouble catching the bar on this move while facing forward, so he started doing it with a twist. Now the move is called a Pegan.

4

Judging and Scoring

It has been said that only a few people in the world are smart enough to truly understand Einstein's Theory of Relativity. Einstein was lucky he went into physics instead of a *really* complicated field like gymnastics.

In the 1932 Olympics, Einari Terasvirta and Heikki Savolainen of Finland were tied for second place after finishing the high bar event. While the judges gathered together to figure out what to do, the two Finns agreed between themselves that Savolainen deserved to win the silver medal and Terasvirta the bronze. The judges decided that was a fine solution.

If only it was *always* that easy.

The judging and scoring of gymnastics is complicated, confusing, and sometimes unfair. Here's just one example: In the four women's events at the 1988 Olympics, Daniela Silivas of Romania finished first on balance beam, first on floor exercises, and first on uneven bars. But the all-around championship was won by Elena Shushunova of the Soviet Union, who didn't finish first on *anything*.

Huh?

"We have the worst judging in any sport," admitted Mike Jacki of the United States Gymnastics Federation after the 1988 Olympics.

It's easy to decide which team wins in basketball—the ball goes through the hoop and two points go on the scoreboard. Whoever has the most points at the end of the game is the winner. In hockey, the puck goes in the net and it's a goal. In track, the athlete who crosses the finish line first is the winner.

But in sports like gymnastics, figure skating, and diving, it's not so easy to decide which athlete is the winner. Judges form an opinion and make the decision. *Human* judges. And human beings have a disturbing tendency to make mistakes.

In some cases, the best man or woman does not win. Gymnastics isn't always fair. Much like life. This chapter will explain the gymnastics scoring system as clearly as possible. Warning—it's still going to be confusing.

SELECTING THE TEAM

In the United States alone, there are fifty-eight thousand competing gymnasts (girls outnumber boys by five to one). A young girl starting out is a level 1 gymnast. As she gets better and learns more skills, her coach will advance her through levels 2, 3, 4 and so on up to level 10. After that come the best in the world, the "elite" gymnasts.

Men, for some reason, start at level 7 and work their way to level 1. But it's the same basic system.

Every year, USA Gymnastics holds about five thousand meets to determine which women and men are the best in the country. The top twenty women and top fourteen men are named to the U.S. National Team. These are the cream of the crop.

They don't all get to go to the Olympics, World Championships,

There is intense competition for the twenty slots on the U.S. national team. But afterward the winners must work together.

Goodwill Games, and Pan Am Games. A few weeks before these big competitions, the top six women and top six men are selected. It is *very* competitive.

The reason the team isn't selected earlier is that a fifteen-year-old's body can change dramatically in a very short period of time. If a girl was picked for the team and suddenly gained fifteen pounds or became injured, it obviously could have a big impact on her gymnastic ability.

SCORING

In competition, each gymnast must perform two exercises in each event. First come the "compulsories," or required exercises.

These are skills that must be performed in a specific sequence with proper form.

For example, on the balance beam, an elite gymnast must execute a perfect cartwheel. On the uneven bars, she must take a series of basic swings to a handstand.

Each gymnastic skill is rated in level of difficulty from A (easiest) to E (hardest). A simple forward roll would be an A skill, for example, while a double twisting Tsukahara vault would be an E. A competition might require a gymnast to perform two C difficulty moves and four B difficulty moves. These ratings of gymnastic skills are evaluated—and often changed—every four years.

Naturally, a beginning gymnast has different compulsory exercises from an elite. In fact, mastering the compulsory exercises is how a gymnast advances to the next level.

Starting in 1997, compulsories will no longer be a part of the Olympics or World Championships. This is partly because they are not considered to be the best indication of skill, and partly because some people consider them to be dull. The sport of figure skating has also eliminated compulsories for top competitions.

The second set of exercises are the "optionals." Here, the gymnast can perform any movements or tricks she'd like (maybe it should be called "freestyle"). Generally, the top gymnasts show their greatness on the optionals. Weaker ones may be just as good, or even better, at the compulsories.

Each event is watched closely by four to six judges, who are former top gymnasts themselves. Each judge gives a score for each performance. The highest and lowest scores are eliminated, and the remaining scores are averaged to calculate the score for that routine.

You've seen gymnasts receive scores such as 9.6, 9.8 and maybe an occasional "perfect" 10.0. This, of course, happens very rarely.

It's harder to get a 10.0 in the optional exercises than it is in the compulsories, because the "ceiling" is lower. Women start with a possible 9.4 points and men 9.0. To achieve a 10.0, they have to perform particularly difficult or original moves so they can earn "bonus points."

If one of the judges gives a score that seems way out of line with the others, the judges will sometimes hold a conference and discuss the scores or review the routine on videotape. Occasionally, they will change a score after holding one of these huddles.

OOPS!

There is, of course, only one way to do a trick perfectly and a

Tatiana Gutsu (1st place), Shannon Miller (2nd), and Lavinia Milosovici (3rd) at the 1992 Olympics.

million ways to mess it up. That's what makes gymnastics so challenging. Even the best gymnasts in the world will almost always make mistakes.

Points are subtracted for poor execution. Whenever a gymnast bobbles, stumbles, hesitates, gets out of control, goes past the time limit, or skips part of her routine, she loses part of a point.

On rings, points are deducted if the rings swing too much or touch one other, the gymnast's shoulder leans on the straps, his feet touch the cables, or he doesn't hold a strength move long enough. On the vault, if the gymnast's legs are apart, elbows bent, or toes not pointed, .1 to .5 will be deducted. On the floor exercises, if a gymnast steps over the line, it's a deduction.

There are penalties for bending the arms while on the parallel bars, bending the legs on the pommel horse, and stopping on the bars. If a gymnast merely takes a tiny step backward to steady herself on a dismount, perfection is lost.

Of course, they lose points if they fall. That is usually disastrous, because the gymnast not only receives a deduction for the fall, but also for failing to complete the trick she was in the middle of when she fell. She does, however, have some time (30 seconds for bars, 10 seconds for beam) to pull herself together, get back on the apparatus, and complete the routine.

Occasionally, you'll see a gymnast who falls receive a higher score than one who remained on her feet. The first gymnast probably did a great routine except for the fall. The second gymnast probably had bad form throughout her routine or committed other infractions that lost more points. That's one reason you'll never see a gymnast fall and quit in the middle of an event. She still has a chance to win.

There are a few other no-nos that lower a gymnast's score: a

Dominique Dawes of the U.S. gets good height, but is slightly off balance. This will cost her points.

dirty uniform, a man forgetting to hook his stirrups around his feet, a woman tugging at her leotard. Gymnasts are told not to shake their heads, roll their eyes, or complain after they get disappointing scores. The judges don't like that and might lower their score.

The quality of elite gymnasts is so high, even the tiniest slip can mean the difference between a gold medal and no medal. To show how close a competition can be, look at the top ten scores in the women's all-around at the 1992 Olympics . . .

1.	**Tatiana Gutsu**	**39.737**
2.	**Shannon Miller**	**39.725**

Alexei Voropayev of Russia displaying perfect form on the "p-bars."

3.	Lavinia Milosovici	39.687
4.	Cristina Bontas	39.674
5.	Svetlana Boginskaya	39.673
6.	Gina Gogean	39.624
7.	Tatiana Lisenko	39.537
8.	Henrietta Onodi	39.449
9.	Christina Fraguas	39.424
10.	Kim Zmeskal	39.412

With such tiny differences in performances, the judges must be nearly perfect themselves. Like the athletes, judges have to qualify for top international events like the Olympics. They are also required to take an oath of honesty to ensure that their rulings are fair to all the competitors.

NO MORE TENS! NO MORE TENS!

After Olga Korbut and Nadia Comaneci shocked the world in 1972 and 1976, gymnasts began doing seemingly impossible tricks that called for incredible strength, flexibility, and endurance. The big moves—flying dismounts, triple somersaults, flying off a bar and catching it in midair—are what makes a crowd let out a collective gasp.

The judges have been playing along, putting more emphasis on daring. Today, gymnasts know they will receive higher scores if their routines are difficult than if they are simply graceful.

Scores have been going up, too. In the 1976 Olympics, the women received 27 scores of 9.8 or higher (the men got 8). In the 1992 Olympics there were 132 scores of 9.9 or higher.

In the gymnastics world, many people feel that high scores are

Some experts believe the judges hand out perfect tens for performances that are less than perfect.

being handed out too easily. Fans have been heard chanting, "No more tens! No more tens!"

NAMING NAMES

In the 1970 World Championships, twenty-two-year-old Mitsuo Tsukahara of Japan stunned the gymnastics community with a new vault. Jumping to the horse, he made a half turn of his body. Then, after punching off the horse, he did a one-and-a-half back somersault before landing.

Nobody had ever seen anything like it. Tsukahara won the gold medal and the "Tsukahara"—sometimes called the "sook"—became a part of gymnastics.

It happens again and again. In the middle of the 1966 World

Mitsuo Tsukahara of Japan became famous for the vault that bears his name, but he was a great all-around gymnast. Here he is doing a double pike dismount from the parallel bars in the 1976 Olympics.

Championships, Sergei Diamidov of the Soviet Union was doing his parallel bars routine. He swung up into a handstand, took one hand off its bar and used his other hand to turn his entire body around. This move came to be called the "Diamidov."

At the 1982 World Cup in Yugoslavia, Natalia Yurchenko introduced an exciting new vault. She did a roundoff onto the springboard, a back handspring onto the horse, and a one-and-a-half somersault off the horse. Say "Yurchenko" to any gymnast in the world today and they instantly know what you're talking about.

The way to win a competition is to show the judges something they've never seen before. Everybody wants to pull off a "killer move" that would have been unthinkable at the previous Olympics. Gymnasts and their coaches are constantly dreaming up new tricks. These tricks are usually named after the person who was the first to perform them in international competition.

Here are just a few tricks that were named after the gymnasts who created them:

Comaneci	Korbut
Connor	Liukin
Cuervo	Magyar
Def	Moy
Diamidov	Shaposhnikova
Endo	Stalder
Garrison	Stütz
Gaylord	Thomas
Gienger	Tkatchev
Guczoghy	Tsukahara
Healy	Voronin
Honma	Yamawaki
Kasamatsu	Yurchenko
Kato	

COMPETITIONS

If you're confused now, here's where it gets *really* tricky. There are three different competitions in a meet:

• The team championship: Each team's five best compulsory scores and five best optional scores are totaled. The team with the most points wins the gold medal.

• The individual all-around championship (or "individual combined"): Each gymnast's compulsory and optional scores for each event are added together. The thirty-six top gymnasts each perform another optional exercise on each apparatus to determine the best all-around gymnast.

• The individual apparatus championship: The six highest scoring gymnasts on each apparatus at the end of the team competition perform on that apparatus one more time. These scores are added to the previous ones and the gymnast with the highest total is the winner on that piece of apparatus.

So a woman could win six medals—one for each of the four events, one for the all-around, and one for her team. Because the men compete in six events, a male gymnast could potentially win eight medals.

THE STAIRCASE EFFECT

All gymnasts are not created equal, and they aren't scored equally either.

Just because a young man or woman makes the Olympic team doesn't mean they have as much chance as anyone of winning a medal. It is an open secret that the gymnasts who go *first* receive lower scores than the gymnasts who go last. It's called "the staircase effect."

The reason for the staircase effect is simple—the judges want to leave a little room at the top to reward a truly spectacular performance. If they give a 10.0 to the first gymnast of the day, what can they do when the next gymnast does an even *better* routine?

This became a problem at the 1976 Olympics. The judges started out giving 9.8s to the beginning gymnasts. Then Nadia Comaneci took her turn and she was clearly much better than everybody else. The judges had to give her 10.0s, and ended up giving her seven of them.

In 1979, two University of Nebraska psychologists did an experiment proving that judges award higher scores if they know that the gymnast is one of the last competitors. So the first gymnasts are actually *penalized* simply because they go first.

Everybody knows about the staircase effect, and coaches base their "batting order" on it. They usually put their most consistent gymnast up first to set a decent baseline score. That athlete should be a team player who is willing to accept a lower score and let somebody else get the glory.

The second gymnast is likely to be the weakest member of the team. The third is better, and the fourth better still.

The best gymnast on the team almost always goes last and is likely to receive higher scores than the first gymnast, even if she doesn't perform any better.

Even aside from the staircase effect, most coaches believe the best *should* go last. When a tight competition comes down to the last vault and the team needs a 9.7 or higher to win, coaches want their best guy or girl on the floor.

A gymnast's score can also be influenced by the team she's on. In general, gymnasts on good teams are rewarded and those on poor teams are penalized. If most of the athletes on a team are scoring in the 8.8 and 8.9 range, the judges are unlikely to give 9.5 or higher to anyone on that team, even if they deserve it. But if the same gymnast was on a team in which everyone was scoring in the high 9s, she would receive a score in that range for the same performance.

Well known gymnasts also score higher than unknowns do, regardless of their skills. It's as if they have earned better scores because they've worked so hard for so long. Judges don't mind slapping a low score on a newcomer.

Coaches try to build their gymnasts' reputations at regional competitions leading up to a major competition. You won't see a complete unknown show up and win a medal at the Olympics. It just doesn't happen.

There's one more thing a gymnast can do to get higher scores— have a terrific warm-up session. In 1991 two Canadian scientists did a study that proved judges give out lower scores to gymnasts who fall or stumble while they're warming up, and higher scores to gymnasts who perform their practice routines perfectly.

It's not fair, but that's the way it is.

KEEPING UP APPEARANCES

Looks count.

You will not find any top gymnasts with purple hair, wild clothes, or pierced noses. They might get a little crazy out of the gym, but they know the judges won't go for anything too different in competition. Gymnasts make certain they are neat, clean, and wear nothing that calls attention to itself. Anything that stands out too much is a distraction, and judges take that into consideration when they put up their scores.

In the 1992 Olympics three gymnasts were penalized because judges felt their leotards were too skimpy. Daniela Bartova of the Czechoslovakian Republic, and Zhang Xia and Lu Li of China received deductions from their scores.

• Hair: Gymnasts don't have long hair. Before the 1980s, most female gymnasts had ponytails or braids. They would tie their hair back somehow to get it out of the way.

Zhang Xia of China was penalized during the 1992 Olympics because the judges felt her leotard was too skimpy.

These days, most have medium length hair that is long enough to pull into a ponytail but not so long that it flops all over the place with the gymnast.

You don't see headbands, combs or hard plastic ponytail holders. If you look closely, you might see a girl with small spring-type clips that match her hair color.

The few gymnasts with long hair twist it into a bun. "If your bun turns out as big as a bowling ball," advises Lynn T. Wilton, a columnist with *International Gymnast* magazine, "it might be time to think about a trim!"

On the men's side, beards and mustaches are extremely rare. The boys, like the girls, are clean-cut and fresh-scrubbed.

• Makeup: Female gymnasts want to present a clean, natural

look. But a girl's eyes and mouth do tend to get lost from the back of the arena, so gymnasts often wear makeup.

Lynn Wilton suggests a little water-based liquid foundation and some blush on the cheeks and top of the forehead. "A heavy hand here and, presto, you're Bozo the Clown, so watch out!" she warns.

Wilton is not opposed to a *little* eye shadow, eye liner, mascara, lipstick, and some powder to keep the shine down. You will see modest earrings in the Olympics too, but nothing too large or dangly.

The idea is to look bright-eyed to the people in the bleachers, but not garish to the judges and other gymnasts.

"Less is more," advises Wilton.

• Clothes: Girls wear simple leotards. Boys wear shorts for floor exercises, and long white pants for other events. In the team competition, teammates wear identical leotards. During the individual events, they can wear different ones.

The rules loosen up for exhibitions. On the Stars of Gymnastics Tour of 1995, Valeri Liukin dressed in jeans, suspenders, neckerchief, cowboy hat, and no shirt while he did floor exercises to the tune of "Achy Breaky Heart." Kim Zmeskal put on a jeweled leotard and poodle skirt while she danced to "Rock Around the Clock."

Gymnasts do not perform in socks, because they would slide on the mat. Some go barefoot, and others wear soft leather shoes or half shoes called "slippers." They have rubber pads at the heel and toe, and allow the foot to bend.

The way a gymnast carries herself is also important. They used to tiptoe to and from the mat like ballet dancers. Then Mary Lou Retton developed a more athletic strut that has been copied by many gymnasts.

Judges like to see smiling, assured, confident faces. They don't like grimaces, tongues sticking out, or extreme displays of emotion. And if they notice that a gymnast looks surprised after successfully completing a trick, they may feel it was luck and lower the score.

LIFE AIN'T FAIR

It has been said that the judging of international gymnastics is like a world war without the bullets. To be fair to all the athletes, no two judges can be from the same country. But using judges from many different countries causes all sorts of problems too. This was especially true while the Cold War was still going on.

"International gymnastics was exposed as a flawed, even corrupt, sport, in which performances take a back seat to politics," wrote *Sports Illustrated* after the 1988 Olympics.

The East German judges were notorious for favoring their own athletes over others, especially Americans. During the 1988 Olympics, Kelly Garrison-Steves of the United States jumped off the springboard to begin her uneven bars routine. Team alternate Rhonda Faehn had been assigned to remove the board, but she was afraid of distracting Kelly so she crouched down on the floor alongside the apparatus.

When Garrison-Steves finished her routine, the East German judge slapped a .5 penalty on the U.S., citing a little-known rule that prohibited coaches from being on the podium during a performance. The United States protested, but it was no use.

As it turned out, the United States finished fourth in the competition—by .3. And who won the bronze medal? The East German team.

"I feel like I was stopped on the highway, robbed, kicked in the mouth, and you go home naked," complained American coach Bela Karolyi (who had defected from Romania and was still learning English). Karolyi has become so enraged at biased judging that on more than one occasion he has led his entire team out of the arena in the middle of a competition.

After the incident, the rules were changed so that only .3 can be deducted from a score if another person is at the apparatus.

There have been plenty of times when the judging of gymnastics was unfair, but the absolute worst display took place in the 1948 Olympics. In one of the women's events, a judge tried to award a gymnast a score of 13.1 out of a possible 10.0!

The judging *is* getting better. In the late 1970s, judges were identified by country for the first time, so they could be held accountable for their scores. If a judge gives an obviously high or low mark these days, the fans let him or her have it by booing and hooting.

Inevitably, there will be situations where the better gymnast does not win. That's one reason why gymnasts should enter the sport because they love it and not solely to win medals and honors.

"Look," said American Missy Marlowe, "if I only did gymnastics for results, I wouldn't put up with all this."

— 5 —

A Day in the Life of a Gymnast:
Amanda Borden

Of the fifty-eight thousand competitive gymnasts in the United States only twenty-four are selected to be on the Women's Senior National Team.

These twenty-four young women are amazing athletes, of course. They have spectacular coordination, flexibility, balance, agility, grace, and strength.

But it takes more than physical skill to get where they've gotten. They also had to have a burning desire to succeed. They've learned how to stay cool under intense pressure. They know how to deal with adversity, and to bounce back from it. They don't give up.

Each of these twenty-four athletes has the guts of a soldier, the concentration of a surgeon, the grace of a dancer, the strength of a weightlifter, and the body of a child.

Most of all, they all share one quality—total dedication. To reach their level of achievement, they had to train almost every day, and sometimes at night, and they attended competitions on weekends. This went on throughout their childhoods. There was little time left over for movies, hanging out with friends, or slumber parties.

Gymnastics is not a sport for kids who like to goof around.

"You give up your childhood," admitted Mary Lou Retton. "You miss proms and games and high school events, and people say it's awful. I don't know. I mean, I walked on top of the Great Wall in China when I was in eighth grade. I rode the bullet train in Japan. I met Gorbachev. I met Michael Jackson. I say it was a good trade. You miss something, but I think I gained more than I lost."

The rare child who makes the Women's Senior National Team has a lot to show for the work she put in. She is in great physical shape. She was able to master *extremely* difficult skills, which has helped her self-esteem. She has the opportunity to travel the world. She has a good shot at winning a college scholarship.

And who knows? She just might win an Olympic medal.

Amanda Kathleen Borden is a member of the United States Women's Senior National Team.

She was born on May 10, 1977, in Cincinnati and began taking ballet lessons when she was very young. During a lesson when Amanda was seven, the mother of one of the other girls told Amanda's mom, Patty, that Amanda was built more like a gymnast than a ballerina. Patty Borden, who works as a medical assistant, enrolled Amanda in a once-a-week gymnastics class.

Her talent showed right away, and within a month Amanda was taking gymnastics three times a week. She improved rapidly, and soon it was six days a week.

At the 1992 United States Championships, Amanda finished fifth and just missed being chosen to compete in the Olympic Games in Barcelona. She was fourth in 1993, and third in 1994. In 1995, she placed second in the Pan American Games. Going into the 1996 Olympics, Amanda was one of America's top gymnasts.

Here is what a typical day in her life was like while she was in high school:

A Day in the Life of a Gymnast: Amanda Borden

Amanda Borden on the beam at the 1994 World Championships. She didn't win an individual medal, but she did get a silver as part of the American team.

5:30 a.m.: It's still dark out. Amanda's dad Doug Borden, a director of surgical services at a Cincinnati hospital, tiptoes into her room and gently wakes her up. It takes him a couple of shoves before Amanda gets out of bed.

"I *love* to sleep," says Amanda, who would snooze ten hours if she could.

She puts on a pair of sweatpants and a sweatshirt for her morning workout. She doesn't wear any jewelry during the day, but will put on small earrings for competitions. She doesn't wear makeup either, except for competitions. In those situations, her coach will apply a little blush.

She doesn't need much. Amanda has blond hair, blue eyes, and a smile that lights up any arena even when she's having a bad day. In fact, her nickname is "Pepsodent."

5:45: For breakfast, Amanda usually has a banana or a Snackwells fat free fruit bar. She is 5 feet tall, weighs 98 pounds, and watches her diet carefully. Her favorite food is tuna, and she also likes tomatoes, pasta, and frozen yogurt. She won't eat anything with a lot of fat in it, and even takes cheese off pizza before eating it.

"My friends will get cookies and give me a bite," she says. "That's usually all I need." It's been years since Amanda last ate ice cream.

6:00: She drives her white Plymouth Neon to the Cincinnati Gymnastics Academy to work out. Before she had her driver's license, Amanda's parents made room in their schedules to drive her around. Sometimes she had to rely on her coach or a carpool.

6:15: Practice begins. Amanda's coach for the last six years has been Mary Lee Tracy. She has Amanda and four other young women warm up with a ten-minute run, and then some stretching. This is crucial. Stretching loosens up tight muscles and increases oxygen and blood flow. Afterward, the gymnasts do sit-ups and push-ups. It's a full body conditioning.

"You're tired in the morning," Amanda says. "It kind of gets you going before you work out."

Amanda and Mary Lee will devote today's workout to the compulsory exercises of one event. Tomorrow morning they'll work on a different event, and the next day another one. Amanda's favorite events are the floor exercise and the uneven bars. She says the balance beam is the toughest for all gymnasts, but she considers the vault her weakest event and the one she has to work on most.

A Day in the Life of a Gymnast: Amanda Borden

8:15: Practice is over. Amanda drives home, takes a shower, and relaxes with another banana or breakfast bar until it's time to drive to school.

10:00: School begins. Many gymnasts don't attend a regular school. They leave home at an early age to train at a gym in another part of the country, taking correspondence courses to complete their educations.

"I don't think I could have done that," Amanda says. "We're a really close family."

She has always attended public school, graduating from Cincinnati's Finneytown High School in June of 1995. She likes math, Spanish, and psychology, while she finds English to be the hardest

Amanda gets a hug for a job well done on the uneven bars at the 1994 World Championships. She is still wearing her grips.

subject. There's one class she has never had to take in school—gym.

Juggling school and gymnastics is hard for everyone. "Sometimes I have so many things going on in my mind that I can't concentrate on what I'm doing," admits Amanda, "but I've gotten a lot better."

She must have. She was awarded an athletic scholarship to the University of Georgia, which was nice enough to wait until after the 1996 Olympics for Amanda to begin her studies.*

In the years ahead, Amanda wants to follow in her parents' footsteps and be a part of the medical profession. She'd like to work with other athletes as a physical therapist, nutritionist, or sports psychologist.

School is over at 3:00. Amanda has a snack (low fat, of course) and drives back to the Cincinnati Gymnastics Academy.

3:30 p.m.: Amanda will do a lot more in her afternoon workout, because it's longer and, as she puts it, "you're a little more awake by that time." Once again, coach Mary Lee Tracy puts the four or five young women through some warm-up and stretching exercises. Then, each gymnast will run through her optional routines three or four times on vault, beam, bars, and floor exercise.

Amanda will also spend some time on the treadmill and stationary bicycle, getting a lot of her reading homework finished at the same time. She has done some weight lifting, but that can be hard on the joints, so her strength conditioning consists of using her own body weight. She will do a handstand and then a push-up from there.

*According to the terms of her scholarship, Amanda cannot earn money from gymnastics. The Bordens have requested that it be indicated that Amanda was not paid for this interview.

(Above) The great Vitaly Scherbo of the Ukraine. The horizontal bar and the floor exercise were the only events he didn't win gold medals for at the 1992 Olympics.

(Right) Brandy Johnson became the 1989 U. S. all-around champion, with the help of her coach, Bela Karolyi.

(Below) American Bart Connor on the "P-Bars" at the 1984 Olympics. He received extra credit for performing on just one bar, and won the gold medal.

(Right) Scott Keswick of the United States. He must hold this position for two seconds, which is a lot harder than it sounds.

(Below right) Before any bars event, gymnasts dip their hands in powdered chalk, which absorbs moisture and reduces friction.

(Right) Ivan Ivankov doing a release move on the horizontal bar. Gymnasts are required to do at least one of these during the twenty-five to thirty seconds they're up there.

(Above) In rhythmic gymnastics people don't perform <u>on</u> the apparatus, they perform <u>with</u> the apparatus. The sport is often ridiculed in the United States, but it is hugely popular in Eastern Europe.

(Right) People can't fly, but Andreas Wecker of Germany comes pretty close. He holds his arms out and his legs together for balance. The higher and farther he soars, the better his scores will be.

(Left) The scissors. The higher the legs go, the higher the score. Male gymnasts consider the pommel horse to be the toughest event.

(Below) If a gymnast leaps for a bar and comes an inch or so too close, she can make a midair correction, and the judges may not notice. But if she's too far away, she could fall and be seriously injured.

(Right) Think you're pretty strong? Try this. For Kurt Thomas, it's easy. On the floor exercise, women perform to music, and their routines are emotionally expressive as well as difficult. The men are expected to perform explosive acrobatics.

(Below) Svetlana Boginskaya's favorite event is the balance beam, but in gymnastics, athletes have to excel in all the events to become champions.

(Above) On a parallel bars routine, the judges look to see if the gymnast's body is perfectly straight, with his arms locked and his shoulders over his hands. It helps to have powerful shoulder muscles.

(Right) Mary Lou Retton took the gold in the all-around by .05 points at the 1984 Olympics. No wonder she's so happy. She needed a perfect ten on her final vault to win, and she nailed it.

She has taken dance classes to improve her grace and rhythm, but in the year leading up to the Olympics her coach has her concentrating on the gymnastic events. Amanda will work with choreographer Geza Posar on the floor exercise. She likes all kinds of music and has performed to such popular songs as "Great Balls of Fire" and "There's No Business Like Show Business."

7:30: Gymnastics is over for the day. Amanda will train thirty-three hours this week, including five hours on Saturday. She has Sunday off. That's when she has the chance to pursue her other interests: swimming, shopping, bicycling, and ceramics.

Some of Amanda's friends are gymnasts, while others have nothing to do with the sport. "They've been understanding that I can't always do things with them," she says. "Even though they know I won't be able to do something, they always call and ask me. They've been really great."

When practice is finished, Amanda drives home.

8:00: Amanda is usually not that hungry after practice, but she is very thirsty. She will have a big glass of water or milk. The rest of the family has usually eaten by this time. Sometimes Amanda will have some turkey or chicken, but she's not a big meat eater and often prefers mixed vegetables or Eggbeaters (no fat and a lot of protein).

Sometimes she'll end with a dessert, a fat-free cookie or angel food cake. She doesn't crave sweets, and feels that she could live without them entirely if she had to.

9:00: It's time to do any homework she didn't get done earlier at the gym. If there's time, Amanda likes to relax and talk or watch TV with her mom and dad. Her brother Bryan was once a part of this group, but he left home in 1992 to attend Ohio University.

Amanda's favorite TV shows are *Ellen; Murder, She Wrote; Rescue 911* and just about anything on the Disney Channel. "I never got to watch cartoons that much when I was younger," she says, "because I was always at the gym after school."

Before going to bed, Amanda will take a shower to wash the chalk off her hands. She'll lay out her clothes for tomorrow, so she can sleep as long as possible without having to rush around in the morning.

10:30: Bedtime

It's not the kind of day every teenager wants, but you won't hear Amanda Borden complaining. Her gymnastic skills have taken her to England, Korea, Argentina, Australia, Germany, France, and Japan. Some of the gymnasts she idolized as a child are now her friends. Svetlana Boginskaya stayed over at her house for a week. She met Shaquille O'Neal.

"It's something that grows on you," Amanda says of her sport. "When I started gymnastics I just did it for fun. I never really thought I would get this far. I never did it because I wanted to be number one. Everything I've accomplished I've done by just having fun. That's the only reason I've stayed in it so long. If I didn't enjoy it, I wouldn't be able to get myself out of bed at 5:30 and go into the gym every day. There are times when I don't want to go to the gym and work out, but I think any athlete experiences that. It only makes you a stronger person when you push yourself through those times."

------ 6 ------
Superstars of the 1990s

A gymnast's career is a short one. By the time the 2000 Olympic Games roll around, all of the athletes profiled on the following pages will probably be retired from competitive gymnastics. There will be a new group of superstars by then. But these are the athletes who have made the biggest impact on the sport in the 1990s.*

-- Women --

SVETLANA BOGINSKAYA

Born: February 9, 1973
Hometown: Minsk, Belarus
Height and weight: 5'4", 90 pounds
Medals, honors, achievements: Svetlana owns three Olympic gold medals, one silver, and one bronze. She was the 1989 World Champion, and many thought she should have won in 1991.

*Some deserving gymnasts are not represented here because it was impossible to get enough background information about them. The Americans included are tops in America, though not necessarily the best in the world.

Did you know?: Svetlana competed for the Soviet Union at the 1988 Olympics. In 1992, with the U.S.S.R. no more, she competed for the "Unified" team. Few gymnasts make it to their second Olympics, but Svetlana made the effort to come back for her *third*, in 1996 as a member of the Belarus team.

Favorite event is the balance beam . . . idol was Nadia Comaneci . . . hides her emotions . . . is elegant, not flashy.

Out of the gym: Spent her childhood summers at a gymnastics camp near the Black Sea . . . has done exhibitions all around the world . . . speaks English well . . . favorite place to visit is France . . . favorite city is Nice . . . has never been seriously injured doing gymnastics, but broke her elbow at age seven running on a slippery floor . . . loves to dance . . . enjoys curling up with a romance novel or Agatha Christie thriller . . . collects stuffed animals . . . has her own apartment on the ninth floor of a building in Minsk . . . says she has no interest in getting married . . . is recognized more around the world than at home . . . has been given two cars but didn't have time to learn to drive, so she gave one to her brother and the other to her parents . . . appeared with Vitaly Scherbo in the B-52s video "Revolution Earth" . . . is interested in modeling.

MICHELLE CAMPI

Born: July 29, 1976

Hometown: Sacramento, California

Height and weight: 4'10", 80 pounds

Medals, honors, achievements: Michelle finished third in the all-around at the 1992 U.S. Championships. After several injuries, she came back and finished fifth in 1993. She was the first American women to do a standing full twist on beam.

Did you know?: Michelle began gymnastics at age eight . . . dislocated her elbow the day before the 1992 Olympic Trials and could not compete . . . surgery was required to reattach her tendon with a screw . . . decided to come back and try for the 1996 Olympics . . . fell from the uneven bars in 1994 and fractured three vertebrae . . . didn't give up, resuming her drive for the 1996 Olympics.

Out of the gym: Michelle named her dog (Bogi) and two cats (Gutsu and Milo) after gymnasts Svetlana Boginskaya, Tatiana Gutsu, and Lavinia Milosovici . . . enjoys reading Stephen King novels, swimming, and horseback riding . . . favorite TV shows are *Saturday Night Live* and *The Simpsons*.

Her mom, Celi, gave up her career to help Michelle's, and dad, Bob, sold his car to support her training . . . parents are divorced . . . Celi fell in love with Michelle's coach, Rick Newman, in 1989, and they moved in together . . . Before the 1992 Olympics, Celi got her a phone and the phone number ended with the numbers 1992. Before the 1996 Olympics, she changed the number to 1996 . . . Celi is a bodybuilder.

Quote: "People are always asking me, 'Don't you wish you could go to football games? Don't you feel like you're missing out?' I tell them I'd much rather go to Italy and Japan and the other places I've competed. I have my whole life to go to football games. But I can only do this when I'm young."

DOMINIQUE DAWES

Born: November 20, 1976
Hometown: Silver Spring, Maryland
Height and weight: 4'9", 82 pounds

Medals, honors, achievements: At the 1993 World Championships, Dominique finished second on uneven bars and balance beam. In 1994, she was fifth all-around in the World Championships. She swept the 1994 National Championships, winning the gold in all four events and the all-around. She won on uneven bars and floor exercise in 1995.

Did you know?: Dominique took up gymnastics when she was six . . . at nine, she'd psych herself up for competitions by writing the word "DETERMINATION" over and over again on a mirror in crayon . . . only coach she's ever had is Kelli Hill . . . was an elite gymnast at eleven . . . was roommates with Shannon Miller at the 1992 Olympics . . . finished twenty-sixth in the all-around.

Out of the gym: Dominique attended Gaithersburgh High School . . . likes math and science . . . middle name is Margaux . . . nicknames are "Dom" and "Awesome Dawesome" . . . was prom queen at her senior prom . . . enjoys diving, soccer, sketching, swimming, gardening, and reading . . . favorite music is rhythm and blues and rap . . . favorite TV show is *Martin* . . . favorite food is pizza . . . dad and mom separated in 1993 . . . has a younger brother, Don, and older sister, Danielle, who goes to the University of Maryland . . . will be attending Stanford.

GINA GOGEAN

Born: September 9, 1977

Hometown: Cimpuri, Romania

Height and weight: 4'10", 86 pounds

Medals, honors, achievements: At 1994 World Championships, Gina took first place on the vault, third on floor exercise, and fourth in the all-around.

Did you know?: Gina started gymnastics at six . . . idolized countrywomen Nadia Comaneci and Teodora Ungureanu . . . took up the sport for the fun of it and then, "I realized I was becoming a good gymnast. I then decided that I wanted to be a great gymnast" . . . floor exercise and uneven bars are her favorite events . . . was the youngest member of the 1992 Romanian Olympic team.

Out of the gym: Gina has visited Japan, Spain, France, and England . . . favorite entertainers are Michael Jackson, Arnold Schwarzenegger, and Jean Claude Van Damme . . . would like to be a gymnastics coach when her career is over.

TATIANA GUTSU

Born: September 5, 1976

Hometown: Odessa, Ukraine

Height and weight: 4'9", 71 pounds

Medals, honors, achievements: Tatiana won the all-around gold medal at the 1992 Olympics.

Did you know?: Tatiana's coaches are Victor Dikii and Tamila Evdokimova . . . Dikii chose her from a kindergarten class because she was faster and stronger than the other girls . . . favorite gymnast is Oksana Omeliantchik . . . known for doing very difficult tricks . . . sees herself as a competitor more than a performer.

Tatiana competed for the Unified Team at the 1992 Olympics. In one dramatic moment, she fell off the balance beam. Her teammate and best friend, Svetlana Boginskaya, put her arms around Tatiana and said, "Don't give up. Keep on competing." Tatiana thought the Olympics was over for her right there, but she came back strong. She needed a near-perfect vault to win the gold medal, and she got it.

*Tatiana Gutsu at the 1992 Olympics, where she won
the all-around gold medal.*

After her Olympic victory, the president of Ukraine gave her family a larger apartment and Tatiana received a car and **340,000** rubles (the average monthly wage is 7,000 rubles).

Out of the gym: Tatiana's middle name is Constantinovna . . . likes art, music, and movies . . . dad, Constantin, works for the railroad and mom, Elena, is a machine operator . . . has an older sister named Ira and two younger sisters, Olga and Marina . . . thought about going into figure skating when she was younger . . . enjoys the ocean and loved Miami when she visited on an exhibition tour . . . likes hot dogs and omelettes . . . paints her fingernails bright red . . . likes to play video games . . . hopes to become a coach someday.

SVETLANA KHORKINA

Born: January 19, 1979

Hometown: Belgorod, Russia

Height and weight: 5'3", 103 pounds

Medals, honors, achievements: Svetlana was second in vault and uneven bars at the 1994 World Championships. She has also won medals at the European Games and Goodwill Games.

Did you know?: Svetlana does floor exercises to *Carmen* . . . expresses emotion on the floor . . . is taller than most female gymnasts . . . has been compared with Svetlana Boginskaya . . . coach since 1986 has been Boris Pilkin . . . first major competition was 1992 Moscow Stars of the World.

Svetlana Khorkina of Russia at the 1994 World Championships. She finished second in vault and uneven bars.

Out of the gym: Svetlana has a good sense of humor and is never at a loss for words . . . loves music . . . loves to eat . . . mom, Lubov, is a doctor . . . dad, Vassily, "works in a Yugoslavian enterprise, but I'm not really sure what kind!" . . . has a younger sister, Yulia, who is also a gymnast . . . favorite place is France, where she's visited five times . . . is learning English, but uses a translator for interviews . . . says she will be at the 1996 Olympics "if I don't grow any more. If I get any taller, I probably won't. I'm growing very fast."

LU LI

Born: August 30, 1976

Hometown: Hunan Province, China

Height and weight: 4'5", 66 pounds

Medals, honors, achievements: Lu won the gold medal on uneven bars and silver on balance beam at the 1992 Olympics.

China's Lu Li at the 1992 Olympics. She struck gold on the uneven bars and silver on the balance beam.

Did you know?: When she was five, Lu was very skinny and her mother wanted her to have some exercise. There happened to be a gymnastics school accepting applications, so she signed up . . . Lu's coaches are Gao Jian and Luo Xe Lian. When she got the first 10.0 at the 1992 Olympics, Gao picked her up on his shoulders . . . appeared at the opening of Li Ning's International Gymnastics Academy in Chatsworth, California.

Out of the gym: Lu enjoys music, TV, and movies . . . favorite movie and TV star is Liu Dao Hwa . . . has no brothers or sisters . . . in Chinese, her name means "earth flower" . . . Since her Olympic victory, she is recognized on the street all the time in China.

ELODIE LUSSAC

Born: May 7, 1979

Hometown: Sainte Catherine lez Arras, France

Height and weight: 4'7", 75 pounds

Medals, honors, achievements: Elodie was the best gymnast in France in 1993 and 1994. In the 1993 Junior European Championships, she took first place in the all-around, uneven bars, balance beam, and floor exercises.

Did you know?: Elodie's coaches are Shi Mao and his wife Xian Lin, who used to coach in China . . . favorite gymnast is Svetlana Boginskaya . . . in 1994, Elodie dismounted from the beam and landed on her face, fracturing a bone. She was conscious afterward and could speak, but has no memory of the fall.

Out of the gym: Elodie grew up in the gym, because her parents owned one in Avignon, in southeastern France. She liked gymnastics so much that her dad built a gym in their home so Elodie

Elodie Lussac of France at the 1994 American Cup.

could practice on weekends. He would make up imaginary competitions for her, complete with awards ceremonies.

SHANNON MILLER

Born: March 10, 1977, in Rolla, Missouri

Hometown: Edmond, Oklahoma

Height and weight: 4'9", 76 pounds

Medals, honors, achievements: Shannon is the most acclaimed American gymnast in history. She owns five Olympic medals (two silver, three bronze) and eight World Championship medals. She is the only American ever to win two straight World Championship all-around titles (1993 and 1994).

Did you know?: Shannon's favorite events are the uneven bars and the balance beam . . . known for keeping her cool . . . dislocated her elbow in a fall months before the 1992 Olympics and had to have surgery . . . longtime coaches are Steve Nunno and Peggy Liddick . . . takes ballet lessons twice a week . . . started gymnastics at age six.

Out of the gym: Shannon attended regular school, North Mid High in Edmond, Oklahoma . . . favorite subject was math . . . is a member of the National Honor Society . . . has hazel eyes . . . very shy and speaks very softly . . . appeared in a commercial for the game Trivial Pursuit . . . likes to read, sew, swim, shop, watch TV, and roller skate . . . favorite food is pizza . . . favorite color is purple . . . has an older sister named Tessa and a younger brother named Troy . . . has a horse, cat (Gizmo), dog (Daisy), some fish and some

Shannon Miller, America's best gymnast ever and all-around World Champion in 1993 and 1994.

gerbils . . . her father, Ron, is a physics professor at the University of Central Oklahoma . . . her mother, Claudia, is a bank vice president and gymnastics judge . . . came home from Olympics to a parade of 15,000 people, and the town of Edmond gave her a new car.

Quote: (When asked how she will handle the pressure of the Olympics.) "A beam's a beam."

LAVINIA MILOSOVICI

Born: October 21, 1976
Hometown: Lugoj, Romania
Height and weight: 5'2", 99 pounds
Medals, honors, achievements: Lavinia was tops in vault in the 1991 World Championships. In the 1992 Olympics, she won gold medals for floor exercise and vault. She was number two all-around in the 1994 World Championships, third in vault, and second in floor exercise.

Did you know?: Lavinia's coach was Leo Cosma, until he defected in 1989 . . . choreographer is Rodica Demetrescu . . . started in gymnastics at age seven . . . idolized countrywoman Nadia Comaneci . . . suffered some ankle injuries, and would go to the gym and help out by playing the music for the other girls . . . favorite event is floor exercise, in which she scored a perfect 10.0 at the 1992 Olympics.

Out of the gym: Lavinia was born close to the border of Yugoslavia, and her grandparents were Yugoslavian . . . dad was a wrestler, mom a volleyball player . . . is a big Michael Jackson fan . . . received 7,000,000 lei ($18,000) from the Romanian government after her Olympic performance.

SILVIA MITOVA

Born: June 29, 1976

Hometown: Sofia, Bulgaria

Height and weight: 5'1", 92 pounds

Medals, honors, achievements: Silvia won the silver in the all-around at the Junior European Championships in 1991 and the bronze in vault at the 1992 European Championships.

Did you know?: Silvia suffered a serious neck injury right after the 1992 Olympics. Training was finished for the day and Silvia asked if she could try a few more double twisting double backs on the trampoline. She fell on her neck, and even though she landed in a pit filled with foam blocks, she had no feeling in her arms. She was rushed by ambulance to a hospital. Two operations were performed, and a piece of bone was taken from her hip to fill a hole in her vertebra. She had to learn how to stand and sit, but eventually recovered. Silvia did not compete again, but went on to do coaching and choreography.

Out of the gym: Silvia's mom, Maja, was seven-time Bulgarian national champion gymnast. Then she joined the circus, where she met Silvia's dad, Zarko, who had also been a gymnast. They became gymnastic coaches, and coached Silvia. When she was a little girl, her parents tried to steer Silvia toward swimming or rhythmic gymnastics, but she wasn't interested.

Silvia also tried figure skating as a girl . . . has two brothers, Zarko and Liubomir, and a sister, Maja . . . Liubomir is a top fencer . . . has taken private English lessons.

Quote: "I can only remember that the anesthetist told me good night, and that I felt like a large weight had been taken off my neck immediately after the operation."

DOMINIQUE MOCEANU

Born: September 30, 1981

Hometown: Hollywood, California

Height and weight: 4'5", 70 pounds

Medals, honors, achievements: 1994 U.S. Junior National Champion, 1995 All-Around U.S. Champion.

Did you know?: Dominique burst on the scene at the 1995 U.S. National Championships in New Orleans . . . She is the youngest gymnast ever to be named to the junior national team, and youngest to win a National championship . . . She is coached by Bela Karolyi.

Out of the gym: Dominique's parents Dumitru and Camelia were gymnasts. They emigrated from Romania in 1980 and settled in California. Dumitru vowed that his first child would be a gymnast. When she was three, he would test her strength by seeing how long she could hang from a clothesline.

Even before she won the Junior National Championship, her autograph read, " Dominique Moceanu, 1996 Olympic champion."

Quote: "I like the attention, but I'm not going to get a big head or anything. It's not going to stop me from concentrating on what I need to do."

ELENA PISKUN

Born: February 2, 1978

Hometown: Bobruisk, Belarus

Height and weight: 4'10", 92 pounds

Medals, honors, achievements: Elena took first place in vault at the 1993 World Championships. At the 1994 Worlds, she finished fifth on vault and fifth on floor exercise.

Did you know?: Elena started gymnastics at age six because a friend was doing it . . . coach has been Valery Kolodinsky from the beginning . . . once broke her nose falling off a trampoline . . . favorite event is the floor exercise, though she doesn't like dancing . . . her gym in Bobruisk is so small that she travels to Minsk before major competitions to train.

Out of the gym: Elena's middle name is Mikhailovna . . . hobby is collecting stickers, which she plasters all over her bedroom door . . . enjoys bike riding, playing computer games, and reading detective novels . . . favorite food is anything with sugar on it . . . favorite music is anything fast . . . favorite colors are blue and violet . . . favorite movies were *Aladdin, Terminator,* and *Bloodsport* . . . enjoys studying algebra, and dislikes geometry and science . . . mother is a bookkeeper, father works in a tire factory . . . has a younger brother named Viktor . . . has a Siamese cat named Niki . . . has been studying English for years and speaks it well . . . will be certified to coach when she finishes school . . . favorite countries she's visited are South Africa and the United States.

Quote: "What I like best is the competition itself. It's work in the gym and it can be very difficult. At meets you get to show what you can do. It's like a holiday. A celebration."

LILIA PODKOPAYEVA

Born: August 15, 1978
Hometown: Donetsk, Ukraine
Height and weight: 4'9", 83 pounds
Medals, honors, achievements: Lilia won the gold medal in

vaulting at the 1994 Goodwill Games. At the World Championships, she placed fifth on uneven bars and second on balance beam.

Did you know?: Lilia got into gymnastics when she was five and her grandmother took her to a gym . . . has been coached by Galina Losinskaya since she was nine . . . favorite event is floor exercise.

Out of the gym: Lilia loves ice cream and chocolate, though she rarely eats them . . . collects toys and stuffed animals, her favorites being an American Mickey Mouse doll and an elephant from France . . . enjoys reading books about travel . . . watches a Russian soap opera called *Tema* . . . wants to become a lawyer.

Quote: "It's boring here. We only train. There's the gym, the hotel where we live, and the cafeteria. There's not much else to do."

KERRI STRUG

Born: November 19, 1977

Hometown: Tucson, Arizona

Height and weight: 4'8", 78 pounds

Medals, honors, achievements: Kerri was the youngest American at the 1992 Olympic Games. She was fourteen, and finished fourteenth . . . She was an event finalist or medalist in the World Championship in 1991, 1992, 1993, and 1994. In the U.S. Championships, she was third in 1991, second in 1992, and third in 1993.

Did you know?: Kerri started gymnastics at three after watching her older sister Lisa compete . . . trained alongside (and in the shadow of) Kim Zmeskal and Shannon Miller . . . said on national TV that she thought she was better than Zmeskal . . . has been with many coaches, most recently Jerry Hinkle and Arthur Akopyan . . . favorite events are bars and floor exercise . . . hardest event is beam . . . has done fifty vaults in a single practice session . . . tore an abdominal muscle in 1993 that knocked her out of competition for eight months.

Out of the gym: Kerri attended Greenfield High School in Tucson . . . plans to go to Stanford University . . . dad is a surgeon and she would like to go into medicine or physical therapy . . . middle name is Allyson . . . likes to ski and paint T-shirts . . . enjoys math and French . . . favorite food is raspberries . . . favorite music is country . . . one of her hobbies, according to the USA Gymnastics Media Guide, is sleeping . . . favorite TV show is *Beverly Hills 90210* . . . admires Tatiana Gutsu and Michael Jordan . . . dad calls her "Care Bear."

Quote: "I've become a lot more responsible, because you have to be. You have to be dedicated, for one thing, to give up your family, and disciplined and stuff. But, you know, you still do everything you're supposed to do, even though you don't have your parents there telling you what to do."

STELLA UMEH

Born: May 27, 1975

Hometown: Marlton, Mississauga, Ontario

Height and weight: 5′1″, 103 pounds

Medals, honors, achievements: Stella won the 1991 Elite Canada competition, and led the Canadian team to tenth place in the 1992 Olympics. She was the only Canadian in the all-around final.

Did you know?: Six-year-old Stella was in the car with her mom when they got lost. They pulled into the Mississauga Gymnastics Club to ask directions. A week later Stella started lessons and she's been there ever since.

Stella's coaches are former gymnasts from the Ukraine, Alex Bard and Svetlana Degtev . . . broke an ankle in 1992 doing a dismount off the uneven bars.

Out of the gym: Stella used to do jazz, ballet, and acrobatic dancing, but gave them up to concentrate on gymnastics . . . has performed the floor exercise to "Ngozi," which was composed for her and is her middle name . . . likes any kind of music that's loud . . . favorite colors are black and purple . . . likes to shop . . . idolizes Whoopi Goldberg . . . enjoys cracking people up and acting crazy . . . when asked to name her favorite food, replies, "Food is my favorite food" . . . older sister Stacey, a former gymnast, choreographs floor exercise routines for her . . . her mom, from Guyana, is a surgical nurse . . . her dad, from Nigeria, an electrical engineer . . . entered UCLA in 1995 . . . wants to become an actress.

Quote: "I don't want to be clumped together with the stereotype that everybody thinks gymnasts are. I just want to be Stella."

KIM ZMESKAL

Born: February 6, 1976

Hometown: Houston, Texas

Height and weight: 4'7", 80 pounds

Medals, honors, achievements: Kim was the youngest U.S. women's champion in history and the U.S. all-around champion in 1990, 1991, and 1992. In 1991, Kim became the world all-around champion, the first American ever. She was just thirteen. At the

Kim Zmeskal concluded her floor exercise with this pose at the 1991 World Championships.

1992 Worlds, won the gold in balance beam and floor exercise.

Did you know?: Kim considers uneven bars her toughest event . . . was one of the first two hundred students to sign on at Bela Karolyi's gym in Houston . . . she was six . . . Karolyi calls her "Kimbo" or "the Little Pumpkin."

Kim was heavily hyped to win *everything* at the 1992 Olympics. She appeared on the cover of *Time* and *TV Guide* the week before the games. Few knew she had suffered a stress fracture in her left leg. Five seconds into the Olympics she fell off the balance beam doing a "simple" cartwheel back handspring. Later, in the floor exercises, she stepped out of bounds. She was in thirty-second place after the compulsories, and finished tenth . . .

There was an incident at the 1991 World Championships when Kim and Soviet rival Svetlana Boginskaya didn't shake hands at the medal ceremony. "I hate her," Kim told *Le Gymnaste* magazine. The

Cold War must truly be over, because Kim and Svetlana trained together at Karolyi's for the 1996 Olympics.

Out of the gym: Kim is the oldest of three children . . . mom works for Mobil, dad is manager of a welding products store . . . middle name is Lynn . . . has blue eyes . . . was only 3'10" at age nine . . . likes *Days of Our Lives* and "Boyz II Men" . . . drives a 1993 Probe.

Kim left school in 1989 and continued her studies through correspondence classes. After the 1992 Olympics, she went back to high school and stopped training entirely. A month later, she missed gymnastics and went back to the gym.

After hearing skater Brian Boitano explain that he was returning to skating because he loved his sport, Kim decided to come back to gymnastics and shoot for the 1996 Olympics. When it's all over, she hopes to go into broadcasting and motivational speaking.

Quote: "Some of my classmates joke about my height but they don't do it to insult me. As long as you keep your chin up and have confidence in yourself, people won't look down on you."

-- Men --

VALERY BELENKY

Born: September 5, 1969
Hometown: Baku, Azerbaijan
Height and weight: 5'5", 134 pounds
Medals, honors, achievements: Valery finished first in the all-around, rings, parallel bars and high bar at the 1990 World Cup . . .

At the 1994 World Championships, he finished fourth in the all-around.

Did you know?: Valery's coach is Alexei Orekhov, who noticed him at school . . . says Alexei has never raised his voice to him in all the years they've worked together . . . favorite event is the pommel horse . . . can hold a cross on the rings for seven seconds . . . says the most important qualities for a gymnast are persistence, confidence, and fearlessness.

Out of the gym: Valery was very strong even as a boy, and hardly ever got sick . . . father liked gymnastics and taught him a lot . . . didn't start formal lessons until he was ten . . . enjoys tennis and swimming . . . mother is an eye doctor, dad a joiner . . . has a sister named Natalia.

Quote: "Without doubt, a 10.0 can't be frozen. The next gymnast should be scored higher if he does better."

TRENT DIMAS

Born: November 10, 1970

Hometown: Albuquerque, New Mexico

Height and weight: 5'8", 150 pounds

Medals, honors, achievements: Trent won the gold medal in the high bar at the 1992 Olympics.

Did you know?: Trent's coach has always been Ed Burch of Gold Cup Gymnastics in Albuquerque . . . favorite event is the high bar.

Trent's lifetime goal was to make the Olympic team. He didn't even think about winning a medal. At the Olympic trials he was so nervous that he couldn't eat or sleep for two days. The same thing happened at the Olympic Games and he was really tired at the beginning of the competition. He had no confidence. But when it came to the finals and he had his last chance on the high bar, he did the best routine of his life to claim the gold. It was the only gold medal the U.S. men or women won in gymnastics.

Out of the gym: Trent enjoys outdoor sports . . . studied marketing and broadcasting at the University of Nebraska . . . left after first year to train full time for the Olympics . . . father, Theodore, was a Golden Gloves boxing champion . . . older brother, Ted, was also a gymnast at the U. of Nebraska.

Quote: "I felt like there was so much pressure, I really didn't think I was gonna be able to compete. I was standing up there and I thought I was literally gonna fall over. I couldn't believe the pressure and all I could think about was, it's just thirty seconds, just thirty seconds."

SCOTT KESWICK

Born: March 3, 1970

Hometown: Las Vegas, Nevada

Height and weight: 5'4", 126 pounds

Medals, honors, achievements: Scott won the U.S. Championship on rings in 1989, 1990, 1991, and 1994. He was the ninth best all-around male in the 1993 World Championships.

Did you know?: Scott started gymnastics at age eight. His family was in Iran because his father was in the military stationed there. His parents signed him up for a trampoline class, and Scott tried gymnastics as soon as he got back to the United States.

Scott's nickname is "Vacs," which is short for Kovacs (a trick on the high bar) . . . coaches are Art Shurlock and Yefim Furman . . . strongest event is rings . . . weakest is floor exercise.

Out of the gym: Fifteen colleges offered Scott scholarships . . . chose UCLA and graduated in 1993 with a degree in applied math . . . lives in Los Angeles with his wife, Michelle Hunt . . . likes to ski, read, watch movies, and ride motorcycles . . . favorite TV show is *Cheers* . . . dad works for an aerospace firm today . . . mom works in a post office . . . has an older sister named Tina.

JOHN ROETHLISBERGER

Born: June 21, 1970
Hometown: Minneapolis, Minnesota
Height and weight: 5′6″, 150 pounds
Medals, honors, achievements: John is a three-time NCAA

John Roethlisberger was the best American male gymnast in the first half of the 1990s.

all-around champion and top American male in 1990, 1992, and 1993. In the 1995 U.S. Championships, he won the all-around, parallel bars, and horizontal bar.

Did you know?: John comes from a gymnastic family. His father, Fred, was a member of the 1968 U.S. Olympic team. Today, he is John's coach. John's sister, Marie, was also a gymnast, and served as the alternate on the 1984 U.S. Olympic team.

John started gymnastics when he was eight . . . favorite event is floor exercise.

Out of the gym: John was born in Wisconsin . . . graduated from the University of Minnesota in 1994 with a degree in international business . . . enjoys playing golf, tennis, and snowmobiling.

BILL ROTH

Born: August 21, 1970

Hometown: Mohegan Lake, New York

Height and weight: 5'7", 172 pounds

Medals, honors, achievements: Placed second in 1994 U.S. Championships. Scored a 10.0 on the high bar at the 1990 U.S. Championships.

Did you know?: Bill started gymnastics when he was six . . . favorite event is the high bar . . . was coached by his father, John, a former gymnast, through high school . . . physically bigger than most gymnasts and has very long arms (he is called "Magilla" and "Neanderthal"), which makes rings his toughest event.

Bill has suffered some serious injuries: a ruptured tendon in his left knee, a torn pectoral tendon. He has had three operations and was forced to miss the 1992 Olympics. His parents wanted him to quit gymnastics, but he loves the sport and came back strong, finishing sixth in the country in 1993 and second in 1994.

Out of the gym: Bill's older brother and younger sister were also gymnasts . . . graduated from Temple University in 1993 with a degree in business administration . . . coach is Temple coach Fred Turoff . . . has an outgoing personality and is always smiling, joking, jumping around and high fiving . . . likes to jet ski and surf in his spare time . . . his girlfriend Christina is a former Temple gymnast, and inspired him to keep going after his operations . . . favorite TV show is *Seinfeld* . . . favorite music group is U2 . . . has a good luck charm, a necklace that a teammate made for him after his surgery . . . wants to open his own gym and share his love of the sport with children.

Quote: "I love to do gymnastics. I would do gymnastics until I was probably eighty if I could. I like to entertain people."

Bill Roth is bigger than most gymnasts. He needs those muscles to move his 5'7", 172-pound frame around.

VITALY SCHERBO

Born: January 13, 1972

Hometown: Kherson, Ukraine

Height and weight: 5'5.75", 138 pounds

Medals, honors, achievements: Vitaly *owned* the 1992 Olympics, when he won gold medals for parallel bars, pommel horse, rings, vault, and all-around. He is the best male all-around gymnast in *history,* according to a list compiled by A.B. Frederick, the curator of the International Gymnastics Hall of Fame (included in the back of this book).

Vitaly Scherbo of the Ukraine—probably the best male gymnast ever.

Did you know?: Vitaly started gymnastics when he was seven . . . won the first competition he entered . . . favorite event is floor exercise . . . doesn't like the rings . . . shows a lot of emotion and personality during competitions, unlike most Soviet gymnasts.

Out of the gym: Vitaly's mom and dad are former acrobats. Today, his mom teaches kindergarten and his dad is a children's gymnastics coach . . . has no brothers or sisters . . . likes to fish, read, and do kung-fu . . . has freckles . . . is honest and outspoken, and will criticize his teammates . . . has a wife, Irina, and three-year-old daughter, Kristina.

After the 1992 Olympics, $25,000 was stolen from Vitaly's apartment in Minsk. Three men were arrested, and one of them turned out to be Scherbo's former teammate Nikolai Tikhonovich. The day before the break-in, Tikhonovich had asked Scherbo to lend him $350. Scherbo did, and was so trusting that he showed Tikhonovich where he kept his money.

Quote: "At the very first practice I pulled myself up fifteen times on the bar. This is to show you how much energy I had at the time. We jumped on the trampoline, ran back and forth and turned head over heels all the time. It all looked like a fascinating game."

GREAT COMEBACKS

In the 1904 Olympics, George Eyser of the U.S. won the gold medal for vault, silver for pommel horse, and bronze for high bar. Not bad for a guy with one wooden leg.

Jennifer Sey fractured her leg after falling off the uneven bars at the 1985 World Championships in Montreal. The next year she was the United States National Champion.

In the 1976 Olympics, Shun Fujimoto broke a kneecap during the floor exercise and still led Japan to the team championship. Fuji-moto dismounted from the rings with a triple somersault. He landed cleanly, scored a 9.75, and then fell to the floor in agony. The doctor who examined him told *Sports Illustrated*, "How he managed to do somersaults and twists and land without collapsing in screams is beyond my comprehension."

It takes a tremendous amount of determination to reach the heights in gymnastics. People who have this personality trait don't quit when adversity strikes them. The story of Dmitri Bilozertchev is "one of the most astounding comebacks in the history of sport," according to *The New York Times*.

Bilozertchev, born in Moscow, was a gymnastics prodigy. Just sixteen years old in 1983, he scored 59.85 out of 60 possible points to become the youngest man in history to win the all-around World Championship. He was expected to dominate men's gymnastics for the next ten years.

Tragedy struck on October 13, 1985, a week before he was to defend his title.

Dmitri was engaged to be married, and he was excused from training for the evening to attend a party for his parents and his fiance's parents. After the party, he borrowed his father's car to get back to training camp. Dmitri had only gotten his driver's license two weeks before, and it was a rainy night. When a passing truck splashed mud on his windshield, he lost control of the car.

The car smashed into a light pole and flipped over. Dmitri's foot was between the clutch and brake pedal. When the car crumpled, the pedals squeezed together and nearly severed his leg below the knee.

When the ambulance arrived, Dmitri had no feeling in his left leg.

X rays showed that it was broken in forty places. Muscles, ligaments and blood vessels were damaged. Doctors debated whether or not to amputate it.

They decided not to cut off the leg, but inserted a steel rod from Dmitri's heel to his knee. He would have to teach himself how to walk again. Gymnastics was out of the question.

In the Soviet Union, Bilozertchev was accused of being drunk, foolish, and immature. He was kicked off the Soviet team (as if he could have competed anyway!) and the government reduced his funding.

But all those things only made him determined to make a come-back. He returned to the gym wearing a cast and worked out on the rings, high bar, parallel bars and pommel horse, using only his arms and shoulders. While his leg slowly healed, he was developing an incredibly strong upper body.

Dmitri stunned the Soviet gymnastics officials when he tried out for the national team in 1986 and proved he was good enough to deserve a spot on it.

At the World Championships in Rotterdam in 1987, he shocked the world by winning gold medals on the pommel horse, high bar, and all-around, plus silver medals on rings and parallel bars.

At the Olympics the following year, Bilozertchev scored three perfect 10.0s, winning the gold medal for rings and pommel horse.

Perhaps the most inspiring story is that of Carol Johnson, a Canadian girl who was born with one arm. She didn't let that prevent her from doing anything, and tried figure skating and playing piano before taking up gymnastics when she was twelve. Her friends called her "Lefty."

Despite the fact that she had just one arm, Carol was able to get on a balance beam and do back flips, aerial walkovers, and a full cartwheel dismount. She represented Canada in the 1976 Junior Olympics, and in 1978 she was second in the nation on beam and floor exercise.

Oddly enough, Carol's gymnastics career came to an end after knee injuries threatened her ability to walk normally. But she never let her handicap get in the way of her sport.

When asked if there was anything she couldn't do, Carol Johnson replied, "No, but if I ever find anything, I'll just work at it until I can do it."

7

The Price of Success

There is trouble in the gymnastics world. Deep trouble.

Eating disorders. Crippling injuries. Pain killers and diet pills. Abusive coaches. Obsessed parents. Zombie-like young women who grow up without a childhood. Suicide attempts. Deaths.

The rest of this book might have made you want to become a gymnast. This chapter might give you second thoughts.

When Olga Korbut mounted the victory stand in the 1972 Olympics, gymnastics was changed forever. For better, and for worse.

Olga changed gymnastics for the better because millions of people around the world were exposed to this fascinating sport for the first time. They could appreciate its beauty, grace, and excitement.

Olga changed gymnastics for the worse because it went from a sport for mature women to a sport for little girls—little girls who are not necessarily ready for everything that goes along with being a top athlete.

How gymnastics has changed. When Vera Čáslavská won four gold medals at the 1968 Olympics, she was twenty-six years

*In the 1960s, gymnastics was a sport for women like Vera Caslavska (left).
Now the best female gymnasts in the world are girls like
Shannon Miller (right).*

old, 5'3", and 121 pounds. When Shannon Miller won five medals at the 1992 Olympics, she was fifteen years old, 4'10" and 79 pounds.

If Vera Čáslavská tried to compete today, she would get laughed out of the gym. The female gymnasts of the 1990s are all tiny, featherweight, and barely in their teens. Grown women simply can't do the tricks that win medals nowadays.

"The smaller girls, the younger ones, they can do more complicated elements," says Svetlana Boginskaya, perhaps the last truly graceful gymnast. "Sport is sport, and the strongest win."

THE ENEMY WITHIN

You don't have to be a physicist to understand that the heavier the object, the harder it is to get it off the ground. Extra weight uses up valuable energy and robs an athlete of precious inches when she jumps. A gymnast spends a lot of time in the air, so she doesn't want one ounce of extra fat dragging her down.

The problem is that a girl's body changes drastically from age twelve to sixteen, the years when she is also blossoming as a gymnast. Her body fat increases, her pelvis widens, she gets taller and her center of gravity moves up. None of these changes help her in gymnastics.

It's an unwritten rule that "women" have to give up gymnastics when they actually start looking like women. Gymnasts, coaches, and judges all know it. Puberty is the enemy of the young female gymnast.

In 1992, Kim Kelly defeated members of the United States

Kim Kelly.

Olympics team in the national championships and the Olympic trials. But she didn't make the team.

"Kim Kelly was the only gymnast who had breasts and hips," explains author Joan Ryan in her scathing exposé of gymnastics, *Little Girls in Pretty Boxes*.

Putting on weight is perfectly natural for teenage girls. There are two ways a girl can deal with it. The first way is to accept these normal body changes, eat a balanced diet, and exercise to stay fit. The second way is to be miserable about her body image, starve herself, stick a finger down her throat to make herself throw up, and take various drugs to keep weight off.

All too often in gymnastics, the second situation prevails. This is the sad story of one girl . . .

CHRISTY HENRICH: AN AMERICAN TRAGEDY

Gymnastics was such a large part of Christy Henrich's life that the license plates on her red Toyota read GMNAST. She was a straight-A student from Independence, Missouri. Nicknamed E.T. ("extra-tough"), Christy was the tenth best female gymnast in the United States in 1988. She missed making the Olympic team that year by .118 of a point.

Christy was 4'11" and 95 pounds, which is not unusual for a sixteen-year-old girl. But one day a gymnastics judge mentioned to her that she would never make the Olympic team unless she lost weight.

From that moment on, losing weight was all Christy Henrich cared about. Food, in her mind, had become a bad thing.

She drastically decreased her calorie intake, eating just an apple a

*Before her tragic death in 1994, Christy Henrich was one
of America's best gymnasts.*

day, and sometimes only a *slice* of an apple. It seemed to work, at
first. Christy won a silver medal at the U.S. Championships in 1989,
and placed fourth in the World Championships.

But her obsession with losing weight caused her to fall into the
traps of anorexia (self-starvation) and bulimia (gorging on food and
purposely vomiting). When the human body doesn't get enough
nutrients, it doesn't produce the hormones necessary for strong
bones, muscle strength, and endurance.

Gymnasts may be able to seemingly defy the law of gravity, but
they can't do it without food. Christy became so weak that she had
to withdraw from the USA-USSR Challenge in 1990. The following

145

year she was forced to retire from gymnastics altogether.

But somehow, in Christy's mind, she had succeeded on one level—her weight was down to 80 pounds.

After she retired from gymnastics Christy no longer had any need to be thin, but her eating disorder didn't go away. Her weight dipped to 75, 70, 65, and then 60 pounds in early 1992. When she tried eating solid food, it hurt her stomach.

"I know I need to eat," she said. "I know I need the nutrition. I know I need it to live. But food is like a poison to me."

Her parents had become alarmed at Christy's weight loss and forced her to check into a hospital. She would be in and out of hospitals ten times over the next eighteen months, but nothing seemed to help. Christy's weight dipped below 50 pounds in 1994.

"My life is a horrifying nightmare," she told a reporter. "It feels like there's a beast inside me, like a monster. It feels evil."

That was Christy's final interview. Her body gave out and she slipped into a coma. Eight days after her twenty-second birthday, Christy Henrich died. The cause of death was "multiple organ failure."

The story of Christy Henrich is not an isolated case. More than half of all top female gymnasts have an eating disorder.*

Cathy Rigby had to be rushed to emergency rooms twice during her gymnastics career. Chelle Stack chugged bottles of laxatives, hoping it would make her lose weight. Nadia Comaneci gained and lost forty pounds within months.

---

* Fifty-nine percent of elite gymnasts admitted they had an eating disorder, according to a 1994 study at the University of Utah. A 1992 University of Washington study found 62 percent of female college gymnasts had an eating disorder. The same year, the NCAA reported that 51 percent of women's teams had gymnasts with eating disorders.

The hottest American gymnast of the mid-1980s was Kristie Phillips. Her picture appeared on the cover of *Sports Illustrated* in 1986 with the headline "The New Mary Lou." Kristie became bulimic, depressed, didn't even make the Olympic team. She said her coach, Bela Karolyi, gave her laxatives and diuretics to keep her weight down. Karolyi denies the charge.

One day, alone in her parents' house after her career had fizzled, Kristie tried to cut her wrist with a scissors. Fortunately, she thought better of it.

Kristie Phillips was touted as "the new Mary Lou" in 1986. Then she became depressed, bulimic, and suicidal.

THE OLDEST GYMNASTS

Years ago gymnasts won medals even though they were over the age of twenty, or even thirty. When she won six medals for the Soviet Union at the 1964 Olympics, Larissa Latynina was twenty-nine years old and a mother. At the 1956 Olympics, Agnes Keleti of Hungary won gold medals on balance beam, floor exercise, and the uneven bars. She was thirty-five.

The oldest gymnast to win an Olympic gold medal was Masao Takemoto of Japan. He won two silver medals and three bronze medals in the 1952 and 1956 Olympics. He was still on the team in 1960, when he was forty years old. He didn't win a medal for an individual event, but Japan won the team championship.

THE MOST DANGEROUS SPORT?

Eating disorders are not the only problem that little girls face when they're turned into top athletes. Though we think boxers and football players suffer many injuries, gymnastics is one of the most dangerous activities a young person can do with her body. Serious injuries are so common that gymnasts consider them all in a day's workout.

Kelly Garrison, a member of the 1988 U.S. Olympic team, went to a doctor to have her hip examined. He discovered she had twenty-two stress fractures in her back. Shannon Miller has a screw in her elbow to hold down a bone chip. Michelle Campi fractured three vertebrae when she slipped off the uneven bars in 1994. She had a rod inserted in her back and spent three months in a body cast.

Young girls grow up fast. Coaches don't always want to wait around for an injury to heal when there are important competitions coming up. It's not uncommon for gymnasts to be shot full of Novocain or other drugs so they can keep on competing.

Kristie Phillips broke her wrist a month before the 1986 U.S. Junior Championships. Instead of giving the wrist time to heal, she took twelve Advils and six Naprosyns a day to deaden the pain. Betty Okino was another "next Mary Lou" before the 1992 Olympics. Then her body started breaking down. She was put on anti-inflammatory drugs, and took eight Advils a day. Today, she can't straighten her arm.

Another gymnast goes down.

GYMNASTICS

Gymnasts sustain more injuries in training than any other athletes except football players, according to a 1992 study done by the NCAA. It's ironic that a sport that was created to promote physical fitness causes so many injuries.

The ankles, knees, back, elbows, and wrists take an incredible pounding in gymnastics. Gymnasts are subject to frequent tendonitis, sprains and stress fractures (bone breaks resulting from the constant repetition of a particular movement).

As gymnastic tricks have become more daring, the problems have become worse. The human body is not designed to soar through the air, twist several times, drop ten feet or more, and slam into its target like an arrow. Certainly not at age twelve.

Take the Yurchenko, for instance. In 1983 Natalia Yurchenko of the Soviet Union introduced a new vault—she sprinted down the runway, did a roundoff onto a springboard, and landed with her back to the horse. Then she leaped backward, pushed off the horse, twisted in the air, and landed on her feet.

Twelve-year-old kids (and younger) are physically able to perform Yurchenkos and other difficult tricks. But their bodies aren't strong enough to withstand that kind of punishment repeatedly. And they're not old enough to realize how dangerous it all is, or stand up and say they're not going to take such risks.

The results have been more than a bad case of shin splints.

In 1989, Puerto Rican champion Adriana Duffy slipped off the horse on a vault at the World Championships. Her legs haven't moved since. Soviet champion Elena Moukina was practicing floor exercises before the 1980 Olympics when she broke her neck. She's a paraplegic today. Fifteen-year-old Kimberly Marinucci of Westbury, New York, fell from the bars in 1986, severely injuring her spinal cord. She can walk, with crutches.

These three were *lucky*.

Julissa D'Anne Gomez of Blue Springs, Missouri, was fifteen years old and ranked thirteenth in the U.S. in 1988. She was competing in the World Sports Fair in Tokyo when she missed a vault and slammed full speed, headfirst into the horse. Her neck snapped instantly. It took three years in a coma before Julissa died in 1991.

The same thing happened to Gary Morava in 1974, when he was twenty-one. Morava was a senior at Southern Illinois University and the 1972 N.C.A.A. vaulting champion. He broke his neck on a botched vault, became paralyzed, and died a few days later.

Julissa Gomez was ranked 13th in the U.S. in 1988. Later she made one small mistake and paid for it with her life.

TOO MUCH PRESSURE

If gymnastics is such a dangerous sport, why don't gymnasts quit?

Many do. After devoting most of their childhoods to their sport, most top female gymnasts retire by the time they reach eighteen. Puberty, injuries, burnout, or the simple understanding that it's time to move on in life are typical reasons.

The girls who don't quit, we would assume, love the sport and have a burning desire to succeed at it. But that's not always the case. Often, girls stay in the sport for the wrong reasons.

Sometimes, a girl's *parents* care more about her gymnastics career than *she* does. Chelle Stack wanted to quit gymnastics, but her mother bribed her to go to practice and threatened to spank her if she didn't. Amy Jackson's father installed bars in their living room and made Amy work out at home.

When a girl's parents are spending $20,000 to $30,000 a year for her training expenses, she's going to think long and hard about quitting gymnastics.

Sometimes, a girl's *coach* cares more about her gymnastics career than she does. He builds his reputation on how many medals his gymnasts win. When she wins, he wins.

Put yourself in his gymnast's shoes. He took you under his wing when you were five years old. He taught you everything you know. For ten years the two of you have been working toward the goal of making the Olympic team. How can you quit on him when the Olympics are just a few years away?

All athletes feel pressure, but there's a difference with gymnastics—there's no room for error. A quarterback can throw the football out of bounds if he's in trouble, and then toss a touchdown on the next play. A baseball player can strike out seven times in ten at-bats and still hit .300. A basketball player can shoot airballs for the whole first half, then come back and be the hero at the buzzer.

Not in gymnastics. In this sport, you start with a perfect score and it's all downhill from there. Points are deducted for every tiny flaw. Kim Zmeskal took one step out of bounds during the 1992 Olympics and it was all over for her. Everything she had worked for during her career went for nothing.

It's no wonder that the gymnasts often look so forlorn at the Olympics. They're too *young* to be under this much pressure.

The funny thing is, even if Kim Zmeskal *had* won the gold medal, there would have been no pot of gold at the end of the rainbow. Unlike other sports, superstar gymnasts are not set for life when their careers are finished.

Olga Korbut and Nadia Comaneci are not wealthy women. After winning the all-around World Championship in 1993 and 1994, Shannon Miller's face was not seen in TV commercials. Mary Lou Retton is the only athlete who ever made a fortune from gymnastics.

"There aren't many endorsements out there for tumbling slippers," says Bart Connor. Few ex-gymnasts can even make a living from the sport when their brief careers are over.

That may change. The popularity of figure skating has skyrocketed in the last few years, and many believe the same can happen with gymnastics. The first World Professional Gymnastics Championship was held in 1991. Once money is a motivation for gymnasts, the pressure to win will be even greater.

A DANGEROUS SYSTEM

Is it any wonder so many gymnasts have problems? Look . . .

• The sport takes girls who are tiny, incredibly flexible, have tons of energy, no fears, and are too young to make their own decisions.

• These girls are put in a gym eight hours a day for a good chunk of their childhood. They're barely exposed to friends, parties, vacations, or normal life. They spend their days repeatedly flinging their bodies around dangerous equipment.

• They are put under the control of a charismatic coach who will scream at them, if necessary, to motivate them. Their parents may push them, make them feel guilty for the money they're spending, or want to live life through their achievements.

• They are required to stay unnaturally thin and childlike, and are sometimes deprived of food or given dangerous drugs.

• They are put in a situation where 50 million people are watching, and any little mistake is disastrous.

• Win or lose, they have to retire while still in their teens. There aren't many financial rewards, and they have few marketable skills except coaching gymnastics.

SOLVING THE PROBLEMS

In a way, the system that developed over the last twenty-five years *works*. It wins medals. Unfortunately, it also creates a lot of young women with serious problems. The question is, what can be done to preserve the excitement, athletic excellence, and beauty of gymnastics without destroying the lives of girls who participate in the sport?

Some things are already being done. Starting in 1997, all gymnasts must at least turn sixteen in the year of the Olympics in order to compete. USA Gymnastics now offers psychological counseling for gymnasts. There are seminars to help coaches deal with their gymnasts' problems.

Other things can be done. Limits could be placed on how many hours a day young gymnasts spend training. The athletes could be required to stay in school until they reach a certain age. Coaches could be certified and required to take courses in child psychology and physiology. Parents could be educated about eating disorders and other problems their children might face.

Judges could base their scores less on daring tricks and more on style and grace. They could also put less emphasis on dismounts, where so many gymnasts get injured.

Two of the world's greatest gymnasts, Soviets Nelli Kim and Olga Korbut, have come out in favor of breaking women's gymnastics into two separate categories—women and girls. "There should be different expectations for someone in a mature stage of womanhood than for a young girl," says Korbut.

Even Bela Karolyi, who discovered Nadia Comaneci when she was six and turned her into a superstar at fourteen, has called for a return to grace and maturity. "It is time for women's gymnastics to reclaim its womanhood," he said in 1994.

If some of these suggestions are followed, we might lose a few medals. But maybe we won't lose another Christie Henrich or Julissa Gomez.

The American men won the gold medal at the 1984 Olympics, but little attention was paid to them.

WHAT ABOUT THE MEN?

The problems discussed in this chapter have not been a big issue for male gymnasts. There's a simple reason—top male gymnasts are *men*, not boys.

The average age of the male gymnasts at the 1992 Olympics was twenty-two years and eleven months. The females were more than five years younger.

Puberty, unfairly, signals the end of a girl's gymnastics career, but the beginning of a boy's. Boys reach this milestone later than girls, at thirteen to sixteen years of age. Their shoulders widen, muscles develop, and their percentage of body fat decreases.

These body changes make a boy into a *better* gymnast,

while the changes a girl goes through at puberty make gymnastics more difficult for her.

The men's-only events—rings, pommel horse, high bar, and parallel bars—require tremendous strength. The women's events require tremendous flexibility. Men are strongest in their early twenties, while women are most flexible in their mid-teens.

The top men, who are often college graduates, are mature and able to make decisions that many fifteen-year-old girls cannot. They're not likely to fall under the spell of obsessed parents or an overbearing coach, as many young girls are.

Male gymnasts are muscular and have developed a positive body image and high self-esteem. Their bodies can absorb punishment. The women are tiny, feather-weight, and *still* think they're too fat.

Last, the men aren't faced with as much pressure as the women. Men's gymnastics is not a glamour sport. When Mary Lou Retton became a sensation in 1984, the U.S. women's team didn't win the gold medal—the *men's* team did! But nobody paid much attention to them.

There have been gymnastic competitions in which the audience actually got out of their seats and moved to the other side of the arena so they could be on the side where the female gymnasts were performing.

Male gymnasts complain about the lack of attention paid to them, but this allows them to compete for the love of it, not just to win medals and please other people.

8

A Timeline of Important Dates in Gymnastics History

776 b.c.: Earliest recorded Olympic Games, in Athens.

a.d. 393: Roman Empire abolishes Olympic Games.

1599: First gymnastics handbook published by Archiange Tuccaro.

1774: Johann Basedow conducts first gymnastics course, in Germany.

1778: Friedrich Ludwig Jahn, "the Father of Gymnastics," born.

1793: Johann F. Guts Muths publishes the first traditional book on the subject, *Gymnastics for the Young*.

1811: Jahn opens first outdoor gym, near Berlin.

1817: Military gymnasium opens at U.S. Military Academy at West Point.

1825: First public gyms in U.S. open in Northampton, Cambridge, and Boston, Massachusetts.

1844: YMCA founded in London.

1856: Princeton becomes the first college to erect a gymnasium building.

1862: Mt. Holyoke College is first college to offer gymnastic instruction to women.

1881: The International Gymnastics Federation, the first international sports federation, formed.

158

1883: Russian Gymnastic Society formed.

1885: The American Amateur Athletic Union (AAU) holds first gymnastic championship.

1888: American Amateur Gymnastic and Fencing Association formed.

1894: International Olympic Committee created, in Paris.

1896: First modern Olympic Games, in Athens.

1903: First gymnastics world championships, in Antwerp, Belgium.

1928: Women compete in Olympic gymnastics for the first time. Holland wins the team drill event.

1932: The floor exercise becomes an individual Olympic event. Tumbling is abandoned as an Olympic event. U.S. wins five gold medals in Olympics. Japanese gymnasts appear in Olympics for the first time.

1934: Gaki Meszaros of Hungary does a split on the balance beam.

1936: Alois Hudec of Czechoslovakia does an inverted crucifix on the rings. U.S. women compete in Berlin Olympics.

1937: George Nissen of Grand Rapids, Iowa, invents the trampoline.

1939: Competitive acrobatics begins in the Soviet Union.

1948: Olympic gymnastics is moved indoors for the first time.

1952: Women compete in individual Olympic events for the first time. Uneven bars replace parallel bars for women.

1959: Spain's gymnastic team is wiped out in an airline disaster.

1962: Rhythmic gymnastics is recognized by the International Gymnastics Federation.

1963: First rhythmic gymnastics world championship is held, in Budapest, Hungary.

1969: AAU and NCAA separate gymnastics from trampoline and tumbling.

1970: Cathy Rigby is the first American to win a medal at the World Championships.

1972: Olga Korbut does the first backflip on the balance beam. Her stunning performance is seen on TV, and children around the world take up the sport.

1973: International Federation of Sport Acrobats is founded.

1974: Music is used with floor exercises for the first time. International Federation of Sport Acrobats holds first world championship, in Moscow.

1976: Nadia Comaneci of Romania is a sensation at the Olympics, winning seven perfect scores. Peter Kormann of Southern Connecticut State College wins the bronze for his floor exercise. He is the first American gymnast in forty-four years to win a medal. Instant replays are used for the first time to help judges.

1978: Americans Marcia Frederick and Kurt Thomas win gold medals in World Championships.

1981: Romanian coach Bela Karolyi defects to United States.

1984: Mary Lou Retton wins the all-around and is the Olympic sensation. Julianne McNamara becomes the first American woman to score a 10.0. U.S. men win the gold medal for best team. Rhythmic gymnastics becomes a part of the Olympics. China participates in Olympics for the first time, winning seven medals in gymnastics, including four golds.

1987: International Gymnastics Hall of Fame is dedicated in Oceanside, California. Sports Acrobatics is officially recognized by the International Olympic Committee.

1991: South Africa enters its first world championship in twenty-five years. Germany's gymnasts compete under the same flag for the first time since 1954.

1995: Liu Xuan of China becomes the first woman to swing a one-arm giant, a move in which the gymnast's body swings all the way around a bar.

——— 9 ———

The Hard Facts
and Strange Trivia

GYMNASTICS TRIVIA

• The leotard was named after nineteenth-century French gymnast and acrobat Jean Léotard. He was the star of circuses in London and Paris. Léotard is also said to have invented the trapeze in 1859.

• Seen in a gymnastics products catalog:

"Stinky Feet????? Pop one of these little plastic balls in each of your shoes. Their scent will fight odor for months. Your gym bag could probably use them too. Assorted colors. $4.00."

• During a Big Ten competition in the 1960s, Illinois gymnast Hal Shaw performed a vault while wearing a Red Baron helmet, goggles, and a scarf.

• During the 1968 European Championships, Larissa Latynina of the Soviet Union was doing her floor exercise when a thunderstorm knocked out all the electricity in the arena. All the lights went out and Latynina continued, illuminated only by flashes of lightning.

• Talk show gymnasts:

In the late 1960s, a guy on the Andover High School gymnastics team in Andover, Massachusetts, was known as "Invincible Jay." Today he's known as Jay Leno.

Dick Cavett grew up in Lincoln, Nebraska, and was a pommel horse specialist in college. He was the Nebraska state champion his sophomore and junior years.

Johnny Carson to Kurt Thomas: Kurt, have you ever had any injuries in gymnastics?

Kurt Thomas: Nothing serious, though I did fracture my neck once.

• At the 1992 Olympics, five of the six Chinese men were named Li.

• Julianne McNamara, who won a gold medal on the uneven bars for the United States in the 1984 Olympics, is married to major league baseball player Todd Zeile.

• In 1949, gymnast Glenn Sundby walked down the 898 steps of the Washington Monument—on his hands. That got Sundby into *Ripley's Believe It or Not.* Today, Glenn Sundby is the director of the International Gymnastics Hall of Fame in Oceanside, California. (If you'd like to visit or receive information about IGHOF, it's at 227 Brooks St., Oceanside CA 92054. 619-722-0606)

• During the 1988 Olympics, the rallying cry of the United States gymnasts was "K-G-B! K-G-B!" (Kick German Butt).

• At the 1904 Olympics in St. Louis, 107 of the 119 gymnasts were Americans. That may be one reason why the U.S. won all seven gold medals.

• A gymnast, Alfred Jochim, carried the American flag at the 1936 Olympics in Berlin. It was Jochim who refused to dip the Stars and Stripes in front of Adolph Hitler.

• At the 1966 World Championships, *two* teams from the United States showed up. The Amateur Athletics Union (AAU) and newly formed United States Gymnastic Federation (USGF) each claimed to represent America. Only the AAU team was allowed to compete, and they finished sixth. The USGF team sat in the stands in protest.

• Not many people would put a pommel horse in their playroom. But if you wanted one, it would cost $1,400 to $1,600. A balance beam costs $800 to $1,500, parallel bars $1,800 to $2,000, and a trampoline runs anywhere from $600 to $2,000.

• When a gymnast takes a fall, the crowd usually goes, "Oooh!" But in Japan, for some reason, the spectators break into giggles.

• In the 1922 World Championships, swimming was added as a gymnastics event. In 1930, the pole vault, broad jump, shot put, 100 meter sprint, and rope climb were gymnastic events.

• The ancient Greeks are known for developing gymnastics, but the sport was also practiced in ancient Egypt, India, Persia, and China. The Chinese used gymnastics in military training. They called it Cong Fu and—you guessed it—it developed into the martial art of kung fu.

• Gymnastics is one of the few sports in which short people have an advantage over tall people. Short bones in the arms and legs can move more quickly. Try swinging a baseball bat and then swing a ten foot pole. The bat is a lot easier to start and stop moving.

Alan Daly, who competed for South Africa in 1991, was one of the few very tall gymnasts. He is 6'3".

• When the Czechoslovakian women's team arrived in London for the 1948 Olympics, gymnast Eliska Misakova took sick and had to be put in an iron lung. She died of infantile paralysis on the first day of competition. The Czech team, including Eliska's sister Miloslava, continued on. Inspired, they won the team gold medal.

- In 1976, a twenty-four-year-old man named Patrick Lajko posed as a high school student so he could become a star on the school's gymnastics team. Lajko had already graduated from Iowa State University when he enrolled as "Scott Johnson" in East High School in Wichita, Kansas. He was exposed when school officials received an anonymous tip.

"I was happy here," he said after he was caught. "The past months at East High have been the happiest time of my life."

- If you wanted to watch gymnastics in person at the 1996 Olympics, the cheapest seats cost $80. For the finals, the best seats went for $212. Scalped tickets cost even more.

- In 1859, a French tightrope walker named Jean-Francois Gravelet (but known as "Blondin") crossed Niagara Falls on a rope 1,100 feet long and 160 feet over the water.

That was the easy part. He was pushing a man in a wheelbarrow at the time.

GYMNASTICS IN THE MOVIES

For a good laugh, get a copy of the 1985 movie *Gymkata*. It stars world champion gymnast Kurt Thomas, who is recruited by the CIA to convince an Asian country they should install an antiballistic missile system.

To carry out his mission (and, of course, save the world), Thomas must survive a deadly gymnastic obstacle course. In one scene, he is seen kicking bad guys while standing on a tombstone outfitted with pommels!

Gymnastics has played a part (though hardly a starring role) in the movies since movies began. In 1897, just two years after motion pictures were first projected on a screen, French gymnasts were filmed doing their routines on parallel bars.

In the silent movie era, film fans could watch Douglas Fairbanks do vaults and one-arm handsprings while swinging a sword in *The Mark of Zorro, His Majesty the American*, and *The Thief of Baghdad*. Buster Keaton was a remarkable athlete who insisted on performing his own stunts. In the 1920 film *Cops*, he performs forward dive rolls down a mountain followed by rolling boulders.

A young man from Newark, New Jersey, named Otto Pohl was an excellent gymnast in the 1920s. One day he was in San Francisco for a gymnastics meet. It happened that people from Hollywood were looking for someone to play Tarzan in a silent movie based on the classic book. Somebody noticed Otto Pohl and signed him up. Pohl changed his name to Frank Merrill and became one of the first movie Tarzans.

In the talkies, you can see Harpo Marx doing back giants on a high bar (but not talking) in *A Night at the Opera* (1935). And there's a wonderful scene in *Singin' in the Rain* (1952) when Donald O'Connor goes absolutely nuts to the song "Make 'Em Laugh."

To see actual footage of early gymnastics, look for *Olympiad,* Leni Riefenstahl's documentary of the 1936 Olympics in Berlin.

Here are some movies in which you can catch at least a glimpse of gymnastics and acrobatic feats:

> *All That Jazz* (1980) . . . *American Anthem* (1985), with gymnast Mitch Gaylord . . . *Annie* (1981) . . . *Babes in Arms* (1942) . . . *The Black Shield of Falworth* (1954) . . . *The Blues Brothers* (1980) . . . *Camelot* (1967) . . . *Footloose* (1984) . . . *The Great Wallendas* (1978), with gymnast Cathy Rigby . . . *Grease* (1977) . . . *If* (1968) . . . *I Was a Teenage Werewolf* (1957) . . . *Rad* (1985), with gymnast Bart Connor . . . *Robin*

Hood (1938) . . . Rock 'n' Roll High School (1979) . . . Seven Brides for Seven Brothers (1954) . . . Teenage Mutant Ninja Turtles (1990, 1991, 1993) . . . Trapeze (1956) . . . West Side Story (1961).

THEY SAID IT

"If I prepare well, I'll get tens in everything and won't have to worry about my competitors. I'll roll right over them like a tank."
—Elena Shushunova, Soviet Union

"When I thought I might have to give up gymnastics, I worried that giving up would then get easier to do everywhere in life, and I don't ever want to do that."
—Tim Daggett, United States

"Gymnastics has been my whole life. It has helped me set goals for myself and become a better person. Because I have to discipline myself and go down to the gym every day, I am happy with myself."
—Cathy Rigby, United States

"Gymnasts execute, in a single evening, acts of greater daring and perform more valiantly more muscular feats than some baseball and football players are called upon to do in an entire season."
—Frank G. Menke, *The Encyclopedia of Sports*

"I wasn't competing against the Soviets. I was competing against my teammates. I wanted to beat them so bad."
—Chris Waller, United States, after the 1991 World Championships. He finished twentieth.

"Young people need a zest for living; healthy sport—gymnastics, swimming, hiking, all manner of physical exercise—should be combined as much as possible with a variety of intellectual interests that will give young people healthy minds in healthy bodies."

—Vladimir Ilyich Lenin, founder of the Communist Party

"I think a lot of people come to gymnastic meets for the same reason they go to the Indy 500. To see exciting, difficult maneuvers and, if they're lucky, to see somebody like me crack up. I don't mean they're hoping I will, it's just that the possibility intrigues them."

—Kurt Thomas, United States

OLD GYMNASTS DON'T DIE, THEY BECOME . . .

• Actors

Mitch Gaylord became a stuntman and took the role of Robin in the movie *Batman Forever.* UCLA gymnast Mark Caso played Leonardo in *Teenage Mutant Ninja Turtles II,* and David St. Pierre of UCLA played a gorilla in *Congo.* Brent Williams of Southern Illinois University was in *Pete's Dragon, Police Woman, Fernwood Tonight,* and *Laverne and Shirley* (playing a tumbler from a Hungarian circus). Buck Taylor was a deputy on *Gunsmoke.* Cathy Rigby performed as Peter Pan on Broadway.

• Circus performers

Olympians Teodora Ungureanu and Eugenia Golea of Romania and Philippe Chartrand of Canada joined Cirque du Soleil, the all-human circus. Rusty Rock, the 1966 NCAA high bar champ, joined Circus Circus in Las Vegas. Bruce Anderson put together a circus act in which he performs one hundred feet above the ground without a net. He also wrote a book titled *The Art of Hand Balancing*.

• Dancers

Michelle Berube, a two-time rhythmic gymnast for the United States, was a dancer on Michael Jackson's "Dangerous" world tour. Sixteen of the twenty members of the Moscow Dance Theater were former rhythmic gymnasts.

• Daredevils

Trampolinist Dar Robinson performed the following incredible feats: Jumped off the top of the Astrodome and landed on an air bag. Parachuted out of an airplane in a car. Did 125 back somersaults in a row.

• Judges

Nelli Kim of the Soviet Union became a gymnastics judge after a career in which she won gold medals on the vault and floor exercise at the 1976 Olympics, and another one on the floor at the 1980 Olympics. In fact, judges at the top gymnastic competitions are *required* to be former gymnasts.

• Coaches

This is the most popular job for an ex-gymnast. Some of them even open up their own gyms. Bart Connor, 1984 gold medalist, runs the Bart Connor Gymnastics Academy in Norman, Oklahoma, and triple gold medal winner Li Ning runs Li Ning's International Gymnastics and Dance Academy in Chatsworth, California.

POLITICS

A few months before the 1968 Olympics, Soviet troops rolled into Czechoslovakia and occupied the country. Athletes from the two nations were able to avoid one another during most of the Olympics, until the women's gymnastics events took place.

In the floor exercises, Vera Čáslavská of Czechoslovakia and Larissa Petrik of the Soviet Union tied for first place. At the medal ceremony afterward, the two champions mounted the podium and stood together on the tiny top step. As the Soviet national anthem was played, Vera Čáslavská bowed her head and turned away.

All too often, innocent athletes have been pawns in the political games played by world leaders. All they want to do is leap, swing, and compete in the sport that they love. Politics, unfortunately, seems to have a way of interfering. This was especially true when the Cold War was still going on.

When the Soviet Union invaded Afghanistan in 1980, the United States and other countries showed their disapproval by boycotting the Olympics in Moscow. Four years later, the Soviets and six other communist countries returned the favor by staying away from the Olympics in Los Angeles. In each case, hundreds of athletes who had trained most of their lives missed their one chance to participate in the Olympics.

Nadia Comaneci was only one of many gymnasts who fled a communist country to seek freedom in the West.

In 1983, Vaclava Navara of Czechoslovakia was on vacation in Yugoslavia with her husband Ivan and son Victor when they saw an opportunity to defect. The family tried to cross the mountains into Austria, but the snow was too deep and they had to turn back.

A year later, they tried again, this time crossing a river in which three other defectors had drowned the week before. Ivan and Victor made it across, but Vaclava was captured and almost drowned. Vaclava was jailed by the Czechoslovakian government. It took newspaper publicity about the family for the authorities to release her.

The family was reunited and settled in Bellevue, Washington. Vaclava's new American friends had a difficult time pronoucing her name, so she now goes by the name Wendy.

With the fall of communism in 1989, there is no longer any need for athletes to defect. Former communist gymnasts are free to go where they like, and many have scattered around the world.

The following classified ad appeared in the December 1991 issue of *USA Gymnastics* magazine:

"Yuri Pavlovich Korozev from the Soviet Union is looking for a gymnastics coaching position in the U.S. Yuri coached Elena Sazonenkova, who was the all-around Champion at the World University Games in Sheffield, England. Contact: Yuri Pavlovich Korozev, Ulitsa S. Lyulina, 28 Apt. #1, Riga, 226069 Latvia, Soviet Union."

In some ways, freedom has made life *tougher* for Soviet athletes. Before the fall of communism, the Soviets developed a gymnastic machine. They won so many medals because the government gave its athletes the best equipment, facilities, coaching, and financial support.

When the Soviet Union crumbled into fifteen independent nations, all that support dried up. Soviet athletes who won medals in the 1988 Olympics were promised nice apartments, but they never received them. The team members were sent off on a world tour and paid as little as twenty-five dollars per show. Elena Shevchenko won a Fiat, but the car was taken away from her because, as it was explained, "fifteen-year-old girls do not need cars."

In 1993, the gymnastic teams from Latvia and Estonia couldn't afford the plane fare to attend the World Championships in England. So they packed into a van and drove fifty-two hours to get there.

OLYMPIC GOLD MEDAL WINNERS
WOMEN

Beam
1952	Nina Botscharova, URS
1956	Agnes Keleti, HUN
1960	Eva Bosáková, TCH
1964	Vera Čáslavská, TCH
1968	Natalya Kutschinskaya, URS
1972	Olga Korbut, URS
1976	Nadia Comaneci, ROM
1980	Nadia Comaneci, ROM
1984	Simona Pauca, ROM, Ecaterina Szabo, ROM (tie)
1988	Daniela Silivas, ROM
1992	Tatiana Lisenko, UNI

Vault
1952	Yekaterina Kalintschuk, URS
1956	Larissa Latynina, URS
1960	Margarita Nikolayeva, URS
1964	Vera Čáslavská, TCH
1968	Vera Čáslavská, TCH
1972	Karin Janz, GDR
1976	Nelli Kim, URS
1980	Natalya Shaposhnikova, URS
1984	Ecaterina Szabo, ROM
1988	Svetlana Boginskaya, URS
1992	Henrietta Onodi, HUN, Lavinia Corina Milosovici, ROM (tie)

Floor Exercise
1952	Agnes Keleti, HUN
1956	Agnes Keleti, HUN, Larissa Latynina, URS (tie)
1960	Larissa Latynina, URS
1964	Larissa Latynina, URS
1968	Larissa Petrik, URS, Vera Čáslavská, TCH (tie)
1972	Olga Korbut, URS
1976	Nelli Kim, URS,
1980	Nelli Kim, URS, Nadia Comaneci, ROM (tie)
1984	Ecaterina Szabo, ROM
1988	Daniela Silivas, ROM
1992	Lavinia Corina Milosivici, ROM

All-Around
1952	Maria Gorokhovskaya, URS
1956	Larissa Latynina, URS
1960	Larissa Latynina, URS
1964	Vera Čáslavská, TCH
1968	Vera Čáslavská, TCH
1972	Ludmilla Tourischeva, URS
1976	Nadia Comaneci, ROM
1980	Yelena Davydova, URS
1984	Mary Lou Retton, USA
1988	Elena Shushunova, URS
1992	Tatiana Gutsu, UNI

Uneven Parallel Bars
1952	Margit Korondi, HUN
1956	Agnes Keleti, HUN
1960	Polina Astakhova, URS
1964	Polina Astakhova, URS
1968	Vera Čáslavská, TCH
1972	Karin Janz, GDR
1976	Nadia Comaneci, ROM
1980	Maxi Gnauck, GDR
1984	Ma Yanhonjg, CHN, Julianne McNamara, USA (tie)
1988	Daniela Silivas, ROM
1992	Lu Li, CHN

Team
1928	HOL
1936	GER
1948	TCH
1952	URS
1956	URS
1960	URS
1964	URS
1968	URS
1972	URS
1976	URS
1980	URS
1984	ROM
1988	URS
1992	UNI

KEY

AUT = Austria. BLR = Belarus. BUL = Bulgaria. CHN = China. FIN = Finland. FRA = France. GDR = East Germany. GER = Germany. GRE = Greece. HUN = Hungary. ITA = Italy. JPN = Japan. NKOR = North Korea. POL = Poland. ROM = Romania. RUS = Russia. SUI = Switzerland. SWE = Sweden. TCH = Czechoslovakia. UKR = Ukraine. UNI = Unified Team. URS = Soviet Union. USA = United States. YUG = Yugoslavia.

OLYMPIC GOLD MEDAL WINNERS
MEN

Floor Exercise
1932	István Pelle, HUN
1936	Georges Miez, SUI
1948	Ferenc Pataki, HUN
1952	William Thoresson, SWE
1956	Valentin Muratov, URS
1960	Nobuyuki Aihara, JPN
1964	Franco Menichelli, ITA
1968	Sawao Kato, JPN
1972	Nikolai Andrianov, URS
1976	Nikolai Andrianov, URS
1980	Roland Bruckner, GDR
1984	Li Ning, CHN
1988	Sergei Kharkov, URS,
	Vladimir Artemov, URS (tie)
1992	Li Xiaosahuang, CHN

Rings
1896	Ioannis Mitropoulos, GRE
1904	Hermann Glass, USA
1924	Franco Martino, ITA
1928	Leon Štukelj, YUG
1932	George Gulack, USA
1936	Aldois Hudec, TCH
1948	Karl Frei, SUI
1952	Grant Schaginyan, URS
1956	Albert Azaryan, URS
1960	Albert Azaryan, URS
1964	Takuji Hayata, JPN
1968	Akinori Nakayama, JPN
1972	Akinori Nakayama, JPN
1976	Nikolai Andrianov, URS
1980	Aleksandr Ditiatin, URS
1984	Koji Gushiken, JPN,
	Li Ning, CHN (tie)
1988	Dimitri Bilozerchev, URS,
	Holger Behrendt, GDR (tie)
1992	Vitaly Scherbo, UNI

Horizontal Bar
1896	Hermann Weingätner, GER
1904	Anton Heida,
	Edward Hennig, USA (tie)
1924	Leon Štukelj, YUG
1928	Georges Miez, SUI
1932	Dallas Bixler, USA
1936	Aleksanteri Saarvala, FIN
1948	Josef Stalder, SUI
1952	Jack Günthard, SUI
1956	Takashi Ono, JPN
1960	Takashi Ono, JPN
1964	Boris Schakhlin, URS
1968	Mikhail Voronin, URS,
	Akinori Nakayama, JPN (tie)
1972	Mitsuo Tsukahara, JPN
1976	Mitsuo Tsukahara, JPN
1980	Stoyan Deltchev, BUL
1984	Shinji Morisue, JPN
1988	Vladimir Artemov,
	Valeri Lyukin, URS (tie)
1992	Trent Dimas, USA

Vault
1896	Carl Schuhmann, GER
1904	Anton Heida,
	George Eyser, USA (tie)
1924	Frank Kriz, USA
1928	Eugen Mack, SUI
1932	Savino Guglielmetti, ITA
1936	Alfred Schwarzmann, GER
1948	Paavo Aaltonen, FIN
1952	Viktor Tschukarin, URS
1956	Helmut Bantz, GER,
	Valentin Muratov, URS (tie)
1960	Boris Schakhlin, URS,
	Takashi Ono, JPN (tie)
1964	Haruhiro Yamashita, JPN
1968	Mikhail Voronin, URS
1972	Klaus Koeste, GDR
1976	Nikolai Andrianov, URS
1980	Nikolai Andrianov, URS
1984	Lou Yun, CHN
1988	Lou Yun, CHN
1992	Vitaly Scherbo, UNI

Parallel Bars
1896	Alfred Flatow, GER
1904	George Eyser, USA
1924	August Güttinger, SUI
1928	Ladislav Vácha, TCH
1932	Romeo Neri, ITA
1936	Konrad Frey, GER
1948	Michael Reusch, SUI
1952	Hans Eugster, SUI
1956	Viktor Tschukarin, URS
1960	Boris Schakhlin, URS
1964	Yukio Endo, JPN
1968	Akinori Nakayama, JPN
1972	Sawao Kato, JPN
1976	Sawao Kato, JPN
1980	Aleksandr Tkachyov, URS
1984	Bart Connor, USA
1988	Vladimir Artemov, URS
1992	Vitaly Scherbo, UNI

All-Around
1900	Gustave Sandras, FRA
1904	Julius Lenhart, AUT
1906	Pierre Payssé, FRA
1908	Alberto Braglia, ITA
1912	Alberto Braglia, ITA
1920	Giorgio Zampori, ITA
1924	Leon Štukelj, YUG
1928	Georges Miez, SUI
1932	Romeo Neri, ITA
1936	Alfred Schwarzmann, GER
1948	Veikko Huhtanen, FIN
1952	Viktor Chukarin, URS
1956	Viktor Chukarin, URS
1960	Boris Schakhlin, URS
1964	Yukio Endo, JPN
1968	Sawao Kato, JPN
1972	Sawao Kato, JPN
1976	Nikolai Andrianov, URS
1980	Aleksandr Dityatin, URS
1984	Koji Gushiken, JPN
1988	Vladimir Artemov, URS
1992	Vitaly Scherbo, UNI

GYMNASTICS

Pommel Horse

1896	Jules Alexis Zutter, SUI
1904	Anton Heida, USA
1924	Josef Wilhelm, SUI
1928	Hermann Hänggi, SUI
1932	István Pelle, HUN
1936	Konrad Frey, GER
1948	Huhtanen, Aaltonen, Savolainen, FIN (3-way tie)
1952	Viktor Tschukarin, URS
1956	Boris Schakhlin, URS
1960	Boris Schakhlin, URS, Eugen Ekman, FIN (tie)
1964	Miroslav Cerar, YUG
1968	Miroslav Cerar, YUG
1972	Viktor Klimenko, URS
1976	Zoltan Magyar, HUN
1980	Zoltan Magyar, HUN
1984	Li Ning, CHN, Peter Vidmar, USA (tie)
1988	Dimitri Bilozertchev, URS, Lubomir Geraskov, BUL, Zsolt Borkai, HUN (3-way tie)
1992	Vitaly Scherbo, UNI, Pae Gil Su, NKOR (tie)

Team

1904	USA
1906	NOR
1908	SWE
1912	ITA
1920	ITA
1924	ITA
1928	SUI
1932	ITA
1936	GER
1948	FIN
1952	URS
1956	URS
1960	JPN
1964	JPN
1968	JPN
1972	JPN
1976	JPN
1980	URS
1984	USA
1988	URS
1992	UNI

WORLD'S BEST ALL-AROUND GYMNASTS
(WOMEN) 1952–1995

1. Latynina, Larissa URS	19. Retton, Mary Lou USA	37. Zuchold, Erika GDR
2. Čáslavská, Vera TCH	20. Roudiko, Galina URS	38. Gogean, Gina ROM
3. Tourischeva, Ludmilla URS	21. Yurchenko, Natalia URS	39. Ashtakova, Polina URS
4. Boginskaya, Svetlana URS	22. Zmeskal, Kim USA	40. Bontas, Cristina ROM
5. Miller, Shannon USA	23. Gutsu, Tatiana, Kutchenskaya, Natalia URS	41. Hellmann, Angelika GDR
6. Shushunova, Elena URS	24. Muratova, Sofia URS	42. Ikeda, Keiko (Tanaka) JPN
7. Kim, Nelli URS	25. Silivas, Daniela ROM	43. Kersten, Dagmar GDR
8. Comaneci, Nadia ROM	26. Szabo, Ectarina ROM	44. Kolar, Trude AUT
9. Bosakova, Eva TCH	27. Voronina, Zinaida URS	45. Korondi, Margit HUN
10. Davidova, Elena URS	28. Milosovici, Lavinia ROM	46. Lazakovitch, Tamara URS
11. Gnauck, Maxi GDR	29. Borcharova, Nina URS	47. Manina, Tamara URS
12. Rakoczy, Helena POL	30. Filatova, Maria URS	48. Onodi, Henrietta HUN
13. Lisenko, Tatiana URS	31. Janz, Karin GDR	49. Pauca, Simona ROM
14. Bicherova, Olga URS	32. Kaleti, Agnes HUN	50. Pervuschina, Irina URS
15. Dobre, Aurelia ROM	33. Korbut, Olga URS	51. Ruhn, Melita ROM
16. Gorokhovskaya, Maria URS	34. Laschenova, Natalia URS	52. Shaposhnikova, Natalia URS
17. Muchina, Elena URS	35. Mostepanova, Olga URS	53. Strazheva, Olga URS
18. Omeliantchik, Oksana URS	36. Petterson, Anna SWE	54. Kochetkova, Dina RUS

WORLD'S BEST ALL-AROUND GYMNASTS
(MEN) 1952–1995

1. Scherbo, Vitaly URS	16. Misiutin, Grigori URS	31. Mogilny, Valentin URS
2. Andrianov, Nikolai URS	17. Tsurumi, Shuji JPN	32. Thomas, Kurt USA
3. Chukarin, Victor URS	18. Belenky, Valery URS	33. Vidmar, Peter USA
4. Shakhlin, Boris URS	19. Kasamatsu, Shigeru JPN	34. Kharkov, Sergei RUS
5. Kato, Sawao JPN	20. Korobchinsky, Igor URS	35. Voropaev, Alexi RUS
6. Korolev, Yuri URS	21. Lehmann, Walter SUI	36. Jing, Li CHN
7. Kenmotsu, Eizo JPN	22. Muratov, Valentin URS	37. Akopian, Artur URS
8. Bilozertchev, Dimitri URS	23. Ivankov, Ivan BLR	38. Deltchev, Stoyan BUL
9. Ditiatin, Alexander URS	24. Liukin, Valeri URS	39. Kroll, Sylvio GDR
10. Artiemov, Vladimir URS	25. Nakayama, Akinori JPN	40. Ning, Li CHN
11. Gushiken, Koji JPN	26. Shaguinian, Grant URS	41. Rove, Olavi FIN
12. Ono, Takashi JPN	27. Tsukahara, Mitsuo JPN	42. Stalder, Sepp SUI
13. Endo, Yukio JPN	28. Adatte, Marcel SUI	43. Tkatchev, Alexander URS
14. Titov, Yuri URS	29. Lisitski, Victor URS	44. Yun, Lou CHN
15. Voronin, Mikhail URS	30. Makuts, Bogdan URS	45. Wecker, Andreas GER

Compiled by A. B. Frederick, Curator, International Gymnastics Hall of Fame

ABOUT THIS BOOK

"What qualifies *you* to write a book on this subject?" Temple gymnastics coach Fred Turoff asked me.

"Nothing," I had to admit.

When I began this book, my knowledge of gymnastics consisted of the words Olga Korbut, Nadia Comaneci, and Mary Lou Retton. So I set out to learn everything I could.

The first thing I did to research this book was to read the last five years of *International Gymnast* magazine cover to cover. This gave me a good basic education about the sport. Next I scanned *The New York Times Index* and read every article on gymnastics that the newspaper ran in the last twenty-five years.

I used *The Reader's Guide to Periodicals* and found dozens of articles about gymnastics in *Sports Illustrated, Life, Newsweek, Time, Psychology Today, People, Esquire, Essence, Science News, American Health, Seventeen, Gentleman's Quarterly,* and *Women's Sports & Fitness.*

Meanwhile, I was calling up experts in the field: gymnasts like Amanda Borden, coaches like Fred Turoff and Rich Tobin, historians like Glenn Sundby and Bruce Frederick, and journalists like Nancy Raymond. Picking their brains gave me a lot of useful information, and they were kind enough to read a chapter or two as I wrote them to point out mistakes and make suggestions.

Finally, I read books other people had written about gymnastics. These are listed in the bibliography.

In writing this book, I learned a lot about this fascinating sport. I hope you found interesting and entertaining information in these pages while you were reading it.

BIBLIOGRAPHY

The Complete Book of Gymnastics, by David Hunn (Chartwell Books, 1979)

The Complete Book of the Olympics, by David Wallechinsky (Penguin, 1984)

Feel No Fear, by Bela Karolyi and Nancy Ann Richardson (Hyperion, 1994)

Gymnastics: A Guide for Parents and Athletes, by Rik Feeney (Howard W. Sams & Co., 1992)

Gymnastics: The New Era, by Mort and Sydelle Engel and Rosanna Hansen (Grosset & Dunlap, 1980)

Gymnastics: A Practical Guide for Beginners, by Tony Murdock and Nik Stuart (Franklin Watts, 1982)

The Illustrated History of Gymnastics, by John Goodbody (Stanley Paul & Co., 1982)

An Illustrated History of the Olympics, by Dick Schaap (Knopf, 1975)

Kurt Thomas on Gymnastics, by Kurt Thomas and Kent Hannon (Simon & Schuster, 1980)

Little Girls in Pretty Boxes, by Joan Ryan (Doubleday, 1995)

Mary Lou: Creating an Olympic Champion, by Mary Lou Retton and Bela Karolyi with John Powers (McGraw-Hill, 1986)

Mary Lou Retton and the New Gymnasts, by Herma Silverstein (Franklin Watts, 1985)

Perfect Balance: The Story of an Elite Gymnast, by Lynn Haney (Putnam, 1979)

Tales of Gold, by Lewis H. Carlson and John J. Fogarty (Contemporary Books, 1987)

The World of Gymnastics, edited by Peter Tatlow (Atheneum, 1978)

INDEX

INDEX

INDEX

INDEX

ABOUT THE AUTHOR

Dan Gutman has written many books for adults and young adults. He is the author of *Ice Skating: From Axels to Zambonis* and co-author of *Taking Flight: My Story by Vicki Van Meter* (both Viking Children's Books, 1995).

Dan is best known for his many books about the National Pastime: *Baseball's Biggest Bloopers, Baseball's Greatest Games, Baseball Babylon, World Series Classics, It Ain't Cheatin' If You Don't Get Caught* (all Viking), *They Came from Centerfield* (Scholastic), and *Banana Bats & Ding-Dong Balls* (Macmillan).

You may have seen Dan's byline in *Sports Illustrated for Kids, Highlights for Children, The New York Times, Philadelphia Inquirer,* and other publications. He also gives talks in schools, where he uses sports to get kids excited about reading and writing.

Dan lives in Haddonfield, New Jersey, with his wife, Nina, and their children, Sam and Emma.